CONTENTS

PREFACE

This book is intended to give an introduction to e-commerce for both new and existing businesses. While it is aimed primarily at those businesses which are already established and successful, there are also specific comments devoted to the 'pure' Internet start-up.

E-commerce or e-business do not mean quite the same thing even though both involve normal business transactions carried out through the new medium of the Internet, or through the World Wide Web, or otherwise electronically. E-business is used to refer to any business transaction carried out electronically. A word-processed document or the use of e-mail are parts of e-business. E-commerce involves procurement, money and the idea of commercial interchange – the relationship between supplier and consumer, buying and selling – on the web. (Terms such as the web, the World Wide Web and the Internet are often used interchangeably; technically this is incorrect (see glossary), but usually it is acceptable.) The growth of this particular sector has been phenomenal and its successes, and (more recently) failures, well documented. Internet launches at the start of the new millennium were running at an all-time high. Millionaires were being made (at least on paper) as Internet-based companies came cap-in-hand to the stock exchange. Most were significantly over-valued, and many have collapsed in a blaze of publicity. Many had been built on the 'new wisdom' that the old rules of business could be discarded. The new economy was set to take on and swallow up the old economy.

Many of these risky start-ups promised new investors a rosy future and an immediate and massive return on their investment. However, a business is not a business unless it can deliver the goods and services which it claims to offer to its customers. The old rules still apply. Businesses are in the business of delivering the right product, at the right place and at the right price for their target market. A failure to address any one of these elements means a failure of the business.

Meanwhile, whilst hi-tech stocks and Internet launches have briefly blossomed and died, a quieter revolution has been taking place in many of the small businesses which already successfully provide goods or services. This book is directed at and dedicated to the proponents and intended proponents of this quiet and increasingly successful revolution – those businesses looking for sustainable, organic growth on the Internet.

Within each chapter there are 'Hints and Tips' boxes to help businesses and 'Did you Know' boxes which highlight current issues. Useful web links have been placed at the end of each chapter. You will also find a brief glossary at the end of each chapter. This is designed for the uninitiated in either business or information technology jargon and explains common terms for those unfamiliar with them. The glossary is collected together at the end of the book. There is also a brief bullet point summary of the chapter content at the end of each chapter.

Glossary

e-commerce   the interrelationship between buyer and seller; commercial interchange

e-business   any business transaction carried out electronically

1 | EMBRACING NEW TECHNOLOGY

'I think I've finally got this technology to work.'

Better late than never is not a rule that can be successfully followed where new technology is concerned! A successful business needs to embrace new technology; it needs to have some sort of Internet presence if it is not to be left hopelessly behind.

Pure dot.coms

There are two distinct and different routes into business on the Internet. The first strategy is to set up as a pure 'dot.com' company (the dot.com refers to the suffix that identifies the business as an Internet company). This means coming up with a sound idea (that no-one else has yet tried successfully) and launching yourself onto the Internet. To emulate the most successful launches you will need to either have money or borrow enough money to get yourself up and running and then convince a high-profile celebrity or business guru to support your venture. This personality will then be expected to endorse the enterprise as you go for a stock exchange listing to raise the capital that you really need to stay in business. If you time this right (and sorry, you've missed out if you haven't done this already) you can become an overnight millionaire with a business that doesn't necessarily have to have actually sold anything – certainly it doesn't need to be making a profit! If you are coming to the Internet now, however, you've missed the boat. Dot.coms have been through a rapid period of growth followed by an even more rapid period of decline.

Figure 1

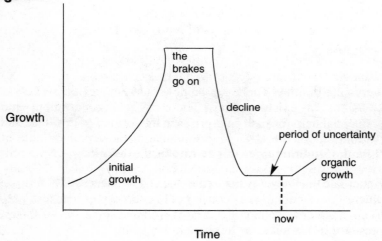

Unrestricted growth could not be supported by the market and rapid decline and loss of confidence followed. The market is now beginning to grow again, but much more slowly and carefully than the first time around.

Fortunes (on paper) have been made and lost almost overnight. There are few (if any) unqualified success stories for dot.com start-ups. Even some of the best known and longest surviving companies have yet to actually make a profit. They depended not only on sales of their own products, but on advertising. Sales have often been slow to grow and distribution has not always fulfilled customer expectations. Advertising revenues were also slow to grow and many advertisers have condemned Internet advertising as ineffective, so that even these streams of revenue can no longer be counted as reliable. What the shake out probably means is that a few companies will survive (and eventually prosper) either because they are big enough to ride the storm, or because they are small enough to have carved out a profitable niche market for themselves. Many, however, will sink without trace (along with the many that already have).

Building on success

The second strategy is the one on which this book concentrates – building on an existing successful business by adding an Internet dimension. This is very much an area of growth where, importantly, levels of risk-taking can be fairly easily minimized. Businesses can create a decent web presence for what is essentially a very small outlay. There can be new markets created as well as extensions of existing ones. There is also government and commercial help for such enterprises in the form of both advice and information. In the UK, government assistance is available at **www.ukonlineforbusiness.gov.uk**. In the USA **www.sba.com**, a site for small businesses, is a good starting point. Telecommunications providers may also be keen to help: **www.bt.com/youcan** will help you create a web site; NTL will help you to upgrade connections to broadband (visit **askntl.com/broadband/default.asp**) and there are many others available.

Some businesses have grasped the concept of the Internet and web-based dealing with both hands. Some have cautiously dipped their toes in the water, and some have adopted (and are still maintaining) a policy of total avoidance. Businesses are at least aware of the net (how could they not be?) but are at different stages of development. Which of the following best describes your business?

- **Victorian**   We offer a traditional service; we rely on personal contact with customers; we write formal letters; we visit customers in their homes or invite them to our premises. We use the telephone and sometimes the fax machine, but all orders have to be received in writing. We aren't against new technology but feel that we don't need it. We have lots of filing cabinets full of paper.

- **Toe-dippers** Our business uses e-mail. Our computers are capable of accessing the Internet but generally we don't bother, after all, the information is usually more easily available in publications. If we do need to go online then, as this stops us from receiving incoming calls, it has to be for only a short period. We really must get round to doing something about this situation.

- **Band wagon** I have to run everything. I want my business to be using new technology but I'm not sure how I should do it. I've organized an Internet connection and have put up a web site, but I don't really have time to maintain it. I seem to get an awful lot of e-mail to cope with, much more than I ever used to get by post. Unfortunately, they didn't introduce IT lessons until long after I left school so I feel that I'm still trying to catch up and always will be.

- **Big Brother** We have Internet access but don't like our employees to use it, after all it can be abused and they are not all that trustworthy; senior staff have better access. E-mail is used for some internal communications but staff must not use it for personal mail. Many staff have their own mobiles but we expect them to switch them off when at work. We don't take orders over the Internet; we keep paper records.

- **New Elizabethan** We use computers which are Internet enabled; we use e-mail for some internal communications. We have a web site run by an in-house appointee who has other responsibilities; the web site gives contact details for the business and we are hoping to upgrade it to take orders. Staff are allowed to access the Internet for business information, and have their own e-mail addresses which can also be used for personal mail. We've even tried video conferencing! We monitor the use of the Internet by staff and know where they've been.

- **New Millennium**   All of our staff have mobile phones and laptops, which they take everywhere – when they travel by train or plane we expect them to work whilst they travel. They can access the Internet using their phone and laptop; we expect them to always be available. All of our internal communications are via e-mail; we book hotels, venues and transport via the web. We keep all our records electronically. We have a professional web site which is maintained by an outside agency. We can take orders and process transactions over the web.

You may not fit exactly into one of these – perhaps you just recognize elements of your business – but many small- and medium-sized enterprises do. How would you rate your own business as far as the Internet is concerned? A leader or a follower? Confident or insecure? Toe-dipper or cutting edge? To build on your business success you need to make sure that your business is e-enabled. Trading electronically should be an integral part of your business. This may mean starting from scratch; it may mean redesigning or re-launching your web site to fit in better with your business; it may mean redesigning your business strategy to take account of your web strategy. In most cases, it means a change to the way that you are currently operating.

Some recent figures from Accenture suggest that the number of users on the Internet has grown from three million in 1997, mainly in the United States, to a total of over one hundred million worldwide. In 1999, it was estimated that there were around 175 million users, with by far the largest slice still in the United States. The bar chart shows the distribution of these. There is still huge potential for growth in the Latin American countries, and Pacific Asia, while Africa and the Middle East are hardly touched at all. Merrill Lynch forecast a Compound Annual Growth Rate (CAGR) of around 25 per cent in the same period. This would give a global market place of Internet users of more than three hundred million early in 2003. The rest of the world is forecast to overtake the United States and have over 55 per cent of the market in 2002. The global commercial market, the Internet and the World Wide Web are not about to go away. They are areas that are going to grow and are likely to dominate many business areas for the foreseeable future.

Figure 2 Figures for 1999 show the enormous growth potential of the Internet

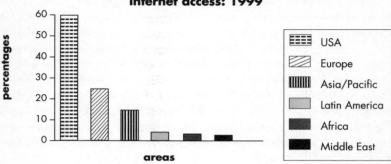

Internet access: 1999

Businesses currently struggling with the uncertainty of the market will, providing they manage to survive the current depression in the sector, emerge as major players in the future of the web. The market will be just as ruthless with e-commerce enterprises as it is with normal ones. Normal business failure runs at a rate of 50 per cent within two years of starting up; a further 25 per cent will fail within five years and e-commerce operations that are inefficient or unreliable, or unresponsive to customers, will quickly find that normal business rules apply. If they can't, won't or don't deliver, then they will fail – probably even more rapidly than they would fail if they can't, won't or don't deliver in the real world.

For small- and medium-sized business there are two main possibilities for expansion on the Internet (leaving aside such things as electronic marketplaces and E2E type business). These are B2C and B2B – business to consumer and business to business (with a third, growing market in business to government, or B2G, as government services are privatized or put out to tender). While the rate of growth has slowed down in both sectors, it is still taking place, and today's growth is more organic. What this means is that most of the growth is both sustained and sustainable, rather than spectacular and doomed to failure. Small businesses will embrace the Internet as an alternative market place for their products and, once the problem of trust has been overcome (between the potential consumer and his or her image of Internet-based trading), transacting business on the Internet will become as normal as going to the Post Office.

The business that is going to succeed in the future on the Internet will need to embrace a number of concepts. Competition means that they will have to sell the best products, at the most competitive prices. There may even be little room for price competition in the long run, and competition may be purely on the basis of non-price competition, especially added value – a difficult but necessary feat to achieve when the seller is not face-to-face with the customer. Further, the successful business will need to attract the customer before the competition, this means a good marketing plan, a realistic and realizable business plan and keeping up with or ahead of changes in technology.

It is essential that the e-commerce business of the future develops a trusted environment, so that the customer is confident of both the security and privacy of his or her transaction as well as of the quality of the product bought. The customer should – as in the high street – enjoy the experience of shopping via the site and want to repeat it on another occasion.

Web links

The UK government offers help to online businesses at **www.ukonlineforbusiness.gov.uk**

and at **www.bt.com/youcan** you can find help on web site construction.

Try **askntl.com/broadband/default.asp** for assistance in upgrading to broadband.

Did you know?

E-commerce businesses are no more likely to fail than ordinary business start-ups. Over half of all businesses established in a year will have failed within twelve months.

Glossary

Business

non-price competition competing through promotions, offers and extras rather than on price

niche market   a small or concentrated part of a market segment

organic growth   slow but sustainable growth of a business

Information Technology

broadband   a faster connection to the Internet

B2C   business to consumer (retailing)

B2B   business to business

E2E   electronic market place to electronic market place

B2G   business to government

Summary

- E-commerce enterprises have been through a period of growth and a period of decline.
- The market is currently recovering from a period of uncertainty.
- Organic growth from inside an existing, successful business, is likely to be more sustainable than explosive growth from new starters.
- Businesses are at many stages with regards to e-commerce.
- The market for Internet transactions is set to grow and continue growing.
- To be a successful business, it is almost inevitable that you will have to trade online.

2 | ADDING VALUE – WHAT BUSINESS IS IN THE BUSINESS OF DOING

No matter how hard you try, if your product is not at the right place at the right time, you will inevitably fail.

Businesses are in business to sell products, or to supply and sell goods or services. The successful businessperson knows that the key to success is to supply exactly what the consumer wants. So much so that one definition of 'quality' is that of customer satisfaction – if the customer is happy then it is a quality product. A quality product is one that is perfectly fitted to its purpose – the purpose for which the consumer has bought it. And the key component in the transaction is, of course, the customer. W. E. Deming, the management guru and 'father' of total quality management, said that all organizations should be 'customer driven'. He further claimed that the customer was 'the most important part of the production line'. The products which businesses offer for sale may be goods (tangible items) or services (intangible items), relatively cheap or extraordinarily expensive, bulky or tiny, fragile or robust, perishable or durable. Whatever the nature of the product, all businesses still have to remember all elements of the marketing mix: the right product, the right price, good promotion and efficient distribution and sales. Business success revolves on having the right product at the right price and the right place for the consumer – and letting the consumer know, through promotion, where and how the product is available.

Keep the rule book

Those commentators who say that this received business wisdom can be discarded because the Internet is a new medium are entirely and utterly wrong. A business which wants to be a success – online or offline – still needs to abide by basic business rules. The Internet may be a new medium through which to conduct business, but that is all that it is. There is nothing in its nature that says that normal business good sense does not apply here. Telephone sales were a new medium when the telephone was invented: have telephone sales led to the death of normal business practice or just enhanced and expanded what was already there? Businesses don't have to have embraced telephone selling as such but it would be a foolish business indeed that did not allow its customers to contact it by telephone. So what do you think is likely to happen with the Internet? Businesses will adapt it and use it and alter it to their own advantage. In only a few years time the term e-commerce or e-business is likely to disappear as the 'e-' part becomes superfluous because it has become such an integrated part of normal business. Doing business on the Internet represents progress. Those who don't grasp the opportunity will be, inevitably, left behind.

The big idea

There are two ways in which you can try your hand at e-commerce. One is to come up with a world-beating idea and launch yourself on to the web as an Internet start-up business. This needs courage, capital and, of course, that big idea (most of the good ones have gone, but you never know...). Many have tried this course of action and have entered into e-commerce with high hopes, succeeding on many occasions in being, if not the best, at least the first in their chosen field. Some were first and have survived – **Amazon.com** and **Amazon.co.uk** are the two biggest online retailers in the world. Amazon launched in 1995 as the first business selling books online; it has expanded into selling everything from CDs to kitchen equipment, but is yet to break even. Others have failed to find the markets they sought. These are the sort of businesses that made headlines at the start of the new millennium, initially for the right reasons, namely successful launch, steady growth and then a stock market flotation to raise the additional capital needed for further expansion.

Letsbuyit.com. was one of the biggest Internet launches of the new millennium. The big idea here was that the business would provide the wherewithal for consumers to band together in order to gain lower prices – effectively to give its members the benefits of bulk buying. There is nothing wrong with this idea, provided that consumers can be persuaded that it will work. The message had to be transmitted to consumers for them to come on board, and so a great deal of advertising and marketing expenditure was needed before it could even begin to generate revenue. A huge customer base was also necessary for it to be effective – this base had to exist on day one, and time spent building it up would be loss-making time. Investors and venture capitalists were quick to see the potential. The markets certainly thought that it could work and it sold some seventeen million shares, valued at one point at over £40.00 each (a market capitalization at its peak in July 2000 of over £800 million). However, by the start of 2001, it had debts of £12.8 million and shares had plummeted to a low of just 17 pence. There was nothing wrong with the big idea, it just didn't take off fast enough or on a big enough scale (revenues of £409,000 in the quarter in which it was floated for £800 million were just not enough) – and markets are fickle – investors will soon find somewhere else to take their capital if they think that they can get a better return elsewhere.

Latterly, as the capital markets have turned their backs on the e-commerce sector due to some spectacular losses, the news has been less good. However, whilst many of the original e-commerce players are categorized by either their fantastic growth or even more fantastic slides, a few, like Amazon, may eventually be long-term success stories. Big versions of such start-ups (with big debts) have tended to implode in a blaze of debt and bad publicity, or been bought and adapted by existing successful (and traditional) businesses for a fraction of what they were once worth; smaller versions have either quietly survived and struggled on, or even more quietly gone under.

But it is not all doom and gloom. Some e-commerce businesses have not just survived, but have thrived. This has been through a combination of providing the right product, at the right price, and one which is easily delivered to the final consumer. (Perhaps one of the most depressing developments is that the most successful businesses on the Internet are, without doubt, those involved in the promotion of pornography. Forrester Research, in a report published in 2000, estimated that American-based Internet sex sites are the fastest growing area of e-commerce, producing over $1 billion worth of revenue with many sites moving into profit within six months of their launch. But look at the features and you'll see why they are successful – easily found and navigated sites offering exactly what the customer wants delivered via the web – they can even sell the same stock over and over again!)

Existing businesses

Alternatively, you are an existing business, successful in your chosen field, who can see the advantages that an Internet presence and capability could bring to all or part of your business. You are not concerned with a pure e-commerce start-up venture, but already have a product and customers. You may not even be particularly aware of the advantages, but have enough nous to see that there must be a disadvantage inherent if a competitor has an online presence and you do not; you can see the sense in providing as many different ways as possible for your customers to contact you or to buy from you. You are reasonably well established, you have some spare capital for investment – or a reliable line of credit – and you are willing to take a calculated risk. You are happy to seek new markets for your products. You are ready for steady but sustained organic growth on the Internet.

An example of such a business is Fox Saddlers, based in the North Yorkshire town of Wetherby in the UK. The company opened its web site before the turn of the millennium and was immediately able to gain customers from any quarter of the world. Unlike **letsbuyit.com** it did not need huge investment in marketing and advertising to attract vast numbers of customers – the business would not have been able to cope with a huge influx from around the world. Customer growth can be steady and change can be slowly introduced as volumes increase. Fox Saddlers targets a niche market of saddles, bridles and other practical horse related products. It relies on quality to sell its products and has, effectively, entered the worldwide markets for saddles. This means that owners in countries keen on horses, such as Spain, Germany, South America, Australia and the Arab states, can now buy online – and the business has sold as far away as Australia. There are many, many more examples of successful small businesses, trading in particular markets. Just go to a search engine and type in a word that describes your own good or service and you will see!

Success and failure

These patterns of success and failure should not alarm the intrepid Internet starter. Similar stories of success and failure are happening all the time – but in ordinary business. There are over three and a half million small businesses in the UK. Indeed 92 per cent of UK businesses are 'micro businesses' with fewer than ten employees; nearly 70 per cent have two employees or less; 13 per cent are one-person businesses. Around 50 per cent of such small businesses traditionally fail or are bought out within their first two years of operation. There is a constant cycle of failure and renewal, with the new businesses often learning from the mistakes of those in whose footsteps they follow. The failure of the so-called dot.com sector has been highlighted because many of these failures have been lumped under the same heading, but they are failures that would have happened anyway. They are certainly not exclusively failures that have been brought about because the capital market's love affair with Internet businesses has ended.

Remember, if you are running a successful business, you have most if not all of the know-how needed to run an e-business. E-business and e-commerce are, after all, nothing more than business and commerce with an 'e' on the front. This means that, far from having to struggle with new ideas and concepts, what you actually have to do is to adapt and adopt your own expertise and experience in a slightly new mode. The basics of business still apply. (How would you, as a business, have reacted had you been around when Alexander Graham Bell made that first telephonic break through? Would you have shunned the new technology, or embraced it enthusiastically, or been a wary but forward looking supporter?) You, the supplier, are making goods and/or services available for other businesses (business to business, or B2B) for local and national government buyers (business to government, or B2G) or for prospective customers/consumers (business to consumer, or B2C). The fact that you can now do this for a fairly basic outlay – even on a very limited budget – means that you can supply the same product or service to a much greater market. Whatever the size of your market segment or particular market niche, you can now immediately reach that same niche on a worldwide basis. If this seems like too much trouble then just ask yourself the following questions about your business:

- Would it help increase sales if you were open all hours of the day and night, seven days a week?
- Are you a business which relies on communication, either with other businesses, with your suppliers, or with your customers?
- Do any of your competitors have web sites or the ability to trade online?
- Do you need or use market research information to support and enhance your business?
- Are you a business which provides customers with after sales service and/or advice?
- How do potential customers know that you exist?

If you answered 'yes' to any of these questions then it is not just likely but inevitable that you can use the Internet in order to enhance and expand your current business. You don't need vast amounts of technical know-how or online experience; you don't need expensive consultants or webmasters. You do need to make some investment – more often in time than in money – to be able to be assured of success.

The product

What about the type of product you sell? Does this have any bearing on your likely success as an e-commerce entrant? Recent figures suggest that the market for home delivery of a variety of goods in the UK is set to continue growing. It was forecast in January 2001 that the figure would double by 2005. (Source: Verdict Research). Many orders are, traditionally, placed via post or telephone, which is why the largest category of goods delivered is clothing and footwear. Almost a quarter of the population has accepted a delivery of this type. Most of these will be through catalogue companies but these have tended to grow at a very flat rate of around 5 per cent. Almost all of the forecast additional growth will come from Internet orders or interactive television. There are still only certain categories of goods which customers are keen to order over the Internet and have delivered to their door. Groceries, for example, despite big supermarket chains opening up web-based ordering systems, have yet to make significant inroads into home delivery.

Other items are limited either by their size, by the customer's wish to try or test the product or by what they cost. The sheer bulk of some items mitigates against their being sold over the web. The cost to deliver say a freezer or a garage door would be likely to wipe out any possible profit. Other items may need to be tried before purchasing. Whilst a customer might, for example, be happy to buy a car stereo over the net, they are likely to be less happy about buying a car in this way without test driving it. Some other products need to be tested by the customer for colour or size. Does this wallpaper really go with my furniture? How accurate are the colour reproductions? Is this a European 12, a British 12 or an American 12? (and is it a big 12 or a small 12?). Size is a problem with clothes and footwear, but mail order firms have counteracted the problem by developing efficient ways of returning items at little additional cost. If you intend to offer such a service, do you have a system for dealing with returns?

So what sort of products do work? The best types are small, portable and not too breakable. A good rule of thumb is to see if the product would work through telephone or mail order. If it does work as mail order then it is likely to translate into a viable proposition on the web. Products such as flowers, chocolates, clothes, books and CDs are good examples of such things and have all been successfully sold over the Internet. As an existing business, it may be that not all of your range of goods or services can be sold in this way – this doesn't mean that none of it can. Usually there is something that you can sell or, if not, something that you can provide, even if it is not for sale. How about, for example, providing free advice to go with the products that you sell?

If you are a business start-up and one that intends to trade online as a primary part of your business then you need to look at Chapter 6 which specifically addresses the peculiar problems and issues that you will face. If you are an existing business, looking to expand on to the Internet, you will face similar business problems to those you would have should you try any sort of expansion. As either type of business you will need to address the following questions:

- How will e-commerce affect the organization of my business?
- How will it affect my people – suppliers, staff and customers?
- How will it affect my processes?
- How do I make strategic partnerships and develop reciprocal relationships to make the best of the opportunities?
- How do I win, and keep, customers' confidence?
- What are the risks and how do I manage them?

Each of these questions is addressed in this book and some have a specific chapter to themselves. There may be other questions which you will need to answer – such as cost and investment of time. It may not be possible for this book to answer those precisely, as they are linked to size, product, staff, rate of expansion, etc., but as a business person you will be aware of their importance.

Adding value

Businesses can be put into two broad categories in terms of the product they supply: those that communicate the value of their product to a customer in order to make a sale, and those where the sales person (or yourself) not only communicates the value of the product, but adds to that value for the consumer.

If you are a seller who only communicates the value of your product or service, the Internet will almost certainly do it better and cheaper.

Indeed, this type of business is likely to be greatly influenced by the Internet. As consumer confidence with online sales inevitably increases, customers will turn more and more to the regularly updated, attractive and interactive catalogues and features which can be found online. This is unlikely to mean the death of the printed catalogue or product leaflet, but is likely to take a greater and greater share of this market. As a salesperson you can tell your customers how good the product is, and you can demonstrate it and extol its virtues, but so can a good web site. It is when your customer starts to ask questions, or goes outside the details printed on the box, that you can become a seller who adds value.

If you are a seller who can add value to your product yourself, then you will be part of that logistical bridge between buyer and seller and the Internet will become a powerful and vital tool for you.*

You are unlikely to see yourself as a salesperson at all, but will be more of a facilitator, one who is in contact with customers and dealing with issues which the customer raises. These may be technical issues – How fast? How far? What size? What else will it do? What do I need with it? What does it taste like? – legal issues, ethical issues, or just providing the customer with the benefits of your experience. Your customers will use the Internet because of the extra value that is added by your advice and expertise.

*With thanks to Tony Sharpe for his insight on added value.

Commercial web sites can also be put into two broad categories. These reflect the different types of business: those where the products are displayed and allowed to sell themselves – a sort of online catalogue known as a feature dump – and those which attempt to persuade the customer to buy through not just the content but the additional services offered. To be a successful e-commerce organization you will need to make sure that your web site is more than just a feature dump and develop it into one that is persuasive through its content. This is a subtle and vital difference. The first venture into Internet selling for many businesses is to put their catalogue online. This is not enough to make you a successful e-commerce organization. The content needs to be attractively presented and to persuade you to buy. Just having a web site is not sufficient. It needs to be a dynamic web site, updated (as an absolute minimum) at least once a month, to lure and attract visitors for subsequent visits and further purchases. It needs always to be current. This is crucial to the success of any online business venture – you must put yourself in a position to add value; you must be prepared to 'sell up'.

Selling up

Think about how a sale is completed in your current offline business. Think about how you have trained your sales staff. Do your sales staff (or you) just say 'thank you' to the customer and allow them to leave with their purchase? Or do you try 'selling up' or adding value? Most successful businesses will admit to selling up. It is the provision of that little bit extra that will either make the customer buy another product, or that will persuade him or her to revisit the business for future purchases. Think of a good waiter who is only concerned (of course) for your well-being. You go into the restaurant for a meal and a member of staff greets you and takes your coat. You are shown to a table and given something to nibble on and a menu. You are already 'locked in' – you will find it much more difficult to leave, even if the service is slow. (Imagine yourself in a queue for food rather than sat at a table – which is it easier to walk away from?) The first thing that you are asked is 'Can I get you a drink?' and the selling up continues. It is not just the meal that you buy but (hopefully) the whole pleasant experience. 'Have you seen today's specials?' 'Would you like extra vegetables with that?' 'Would you like coffee?' – the selling up continues throughout the meal, and the waiting and other staff continue to add value. Do they remember your name? Do they exhort you to 'come again soon'? In short, do they make you feel special? If they do, of course you will come again, and their business is ensured of further sales. There is a subtle balance to strike between this and the 'overkill' that can put customers off. Staff need to know when to let a customer browse and when to try to close a sale. This means having a good knowledge of your customers – much easier in a traditional set-up than in an electronic one where you are not face to face with the customer. How well have you trained your sales staff to add value to a sale? 'Would you like to try our new range?' 'We recommend this widget with that grommet.' 'You'll need one of these.' Even the supermarket tricks of buy one get one free, half-price next purchase and loyalty cards are all ways of selling up. This is what the successful business needs to do on the Internet – to add value to the purchase and encourage the customer to return again and again.

Factors for success

It is worth looking at the sort of factors that are held in common by those businesses that have survived (and even prospered) and those that have not. This will give you some ideas of the pitfalls to avoid. Successful Internet businesses tend to operate in specialist markets (such as Fox Saddlers, see page 13) where it is difficult for competitors to gain a market foothold as opposed to going into markets where low levels of expertise or experience are needed. If you can be successful in a market which it is easy to enter, then so can all of your potential competitors. Management expertise and experience is also an important factor. Managers who know business tend to succeed, while those who know the Internet (but don't necessarily know business) tend to overstretch their businesses and consequently fail. Managers with experience (especially financial managers) know that they need to keep costs under control and will be wary of high spending on advertising and marketing campaigns; experienced marketing managers will know how effective proposed advertising is likely to be. If you spend more on advertising and marketing than the revenue that you receive from sales, you are well on your way to becoming a business fatality. Experienced financial managers will also know that 'spending long' to 'expand short' is not a viable option. If your business finds that it is having to spend its cash reserves in order to stay afloat (surviving in the short term, even, rather than expanding) then it is unlikely to survive.

! | **Hints and tips!**

The key to success in sales is to be able to add value. This means offering the customer more than they actually came for, and encouraging them to return. How do you add value now, for your existing customers? How can this be translated into added value on the web?

? | **Did you know?**

What sells online? In Britain Internet grocery shopping accounts for just 0.4% of the market; in the United States, this is even less at 0.33% whilst in Germany it falls to an even more insignificant 0.1%. Datamonitor estimates that the online grocery market is worth $3.5 billion and will grow into the largest B2C sector as suppliers expand (Tesco.com plans expansion in the Far East; woolworths.co.nz (New Zealand) is doing well) and customers grow in confidence.

Web links

The Federation of Small Businesses site, for small- and medium-sized enterprises (SMEs), can be found at **www.fsb.org.uk**. Other specialist sites exist for those who wish to discuss problems that SMEs may have, ask questions and get answers; the discussion group at **www.virginbis.net** is moderated (i.e. answers to questions and items for discussion are filtered).

Successful small firms include Fox Saddlers at **www.foxsaddlers.co.uk**, and **Amazon.com** and **Amazon.co.uk** now sell much more than books.

Glossary

Business

new economy   businesses which are involved in computers and information technology; businesses which have embraced new e-technology

old economy   everybody else in business (particularly used to refer to staid 'old' businesses such as banking and insurance – although many have grasped new technology more readily than others)

quality   a product that is perfectly fitted to its purpose

Deming, W. E. (1900–93)   American engineer hailed as the 'father' of quality management

TQM (Total Quality Management)   a culture where everyone in an organization is responsible for quality, not just a designated few

micro-businesses   a European Union definition of those businesses with fewer than ten employees

adding value   persuading customers to buy more than they had originally intended; encouraging return custom; also called 'selling up'

Information Technology

e-electronic   can be (and often is) used to prefix almost anything, e.g. e-commerce, e-business, e-tailing

e-enabled   a business's ability to buy and sell or complete other business and commercial transactions through electronic means

Internet   the global network of computers which carries out a number of functions including electronic communications, file transfer, and the hosting of the World Wide Web

World Wide Web   a series of interlinked information pages

Summary

- There has been spectacular growth on the Internet, and some equally spectacular failures. This does not mean that the whole sector should be avoided.

- There are many successful businesses on the Internet. Some are pure e-commerce start-ups (such as **Amazon.com**) while others are expansions of existing businesses.

- A presence on the Internet is not just desirable, but probably essential.

- Businesses should not be afraid of the Internet but merely regard it as a new medium through which to sell.

- Careful slow growth in the new medium is better than the instability that can come about with overly-fast growth.

- The future of selling is on the Internet and inextricably bound up with the concept of 'selling up'; while many products may not be viable for sales over the Internet, adding value is always viable.

- There are common factors which characterize the success and failure of e-businesses.

- Getting your business electronically up to speed is not particularly expensive or difficult, it is essential.

3 | WHAT IS E-COMMERCE?

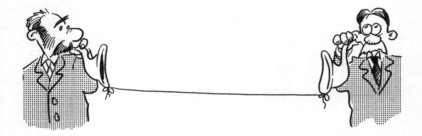

'I can't see this ever developing into anything useful, Watson.'

Definition

By the time you read this it is inevitable that the definition of e-commerce will have widened even further, and the associated technology will have developed new levels of sophistication. Over the past few years the speed of growth of new technology has become faster and faster, with new inventions and adaptations being unveiled on almost a daily basis. Technology that was 'top of the range' only a few months ago will have been superseded by something which does even more, even faster, but which will just as quickly be overtaken. All allow both personal and commercial business to take place over new media. Whatever does take place – from sending greetings to selling products – seems destined to have the 'e-' tag placed in front of it.

This means that you will be operating in an increasingly globalized market. You already have a head start if you are operating in the English language – this is the language common to most of the web – and if you understand how truly global some elements of business have become. Consider how far globalization has progressed in communications alone. Imagine that you are calling up to check on your bank account, or to arrange insurance, or to book a holiday. Whether you ring from Bangor in Wales or Bangor in Maine, you are just as likely to be connected to Bangalore, India! The cost of communications has fallen to such an extent that many companies now site their operations where there is a good standard of education but where the labour charges are lowest, such as India. Your e-commerce venture will be based on cheap and reliable communications. If companies like these can do it, so can you! One thing that is important is to try to keep up with the latest developments. You may not be able to make use of some of them immediately but should incorporate them whenever you are able. They may provide solutions to problems and open up new opportunities for business.

E-business or e-commerce?

So what is e-commerce? The 'e' just stands for electronic and can be happily placed in front of almost any other word describing a possible part of business (or non-business) activity. E-trading, e-tailing (retailing), e-charts (for music), e-travel and e-business are just a few of the terms that have grown along with e-commerce. E-business is basically business transactions which take place electronically. E-commerce describes the interface between business and customer, whether that customer be a consumer, another business or a government body.

Business was only just beginning to cope with much that was new about these procedures when a completely new technology came along. The old electronic means were developing fast: fax machines that combined with telephones, telephone answering machines (which rapidly became ubiquitous) and services such as call diversion had enjoyed growth. But new, faster, cheaper computer technology succeeded in replacing or enhancing much of this. In the communications field, the technology exploded through early versions of e-mail; advances since then have been on a geometrically expanding scale so that it is true to say that the best time to buy a new computer or to update your system is always 'next month'. Whatever you buy today will swiftly be overtaken by something faster, more sophisticated, with greater storage capacity – and often cheaper into the bargain. Hardware, software and peripherals have become more and more efficient as different strands of technology have developed.

Some of the new innovations will work alongside existing kit and systems, while others need to stand on their own. Some are extremely expensive and require much time and thought before a business decides to invest in them; others are cheap, and in some cases free. There are already numerous sites on the web both selling and giving away software so that you can take best advantage of new developments as they come along and without charge.

But don't throw the old technology away! Remember that clients and customers may not be as 'tooled up' as you are and could still be relying on old technology. Fax machines will be around for a long time to come (even though computers can be enabled to send and receive faxes) and the telephone is hardly obsolete! Many businesses have made the mistake of 'upgrading' everything and then discovering either that the new systems don't work properly (many systems need real-time operation before faults and problems occur and can be ironed out) or that suppliers and customers cannot work with new systems. If you intend to replace your old systems completely, then it is a good idea to do it gradually and gently, whilst introducing and testing the new systems. The UK Post Office recently completed a programme of computerizing all of its branch operations. Anecdotal evidence suggests that this changeover has led to slower service and confusion in a number of cases. However, in the long run, the service will undoubtedly be slicker and better. The mistake was to go straight to the computerized system with no intervening period of transition.

Technological development

Development has taken place centred on different technologies –
communications (particularly mobile phones), miniaturization
(e.g. tiny cameras), digitalization (producing better music and
picture quality) and portability (laptops and PDAs) are just some of
the driving forces. Different technologies have been approached
from different directions and will, inevitably, merge. The main
technological strands include both personal and commercial
applications. For example, your supermarket shopping has its bar
codes electronically scanned, which passes information
electronically so that stock can be replenished; your money is then
taken electronically from your bank and transferred to the
supermarket's accounts. Systems used include EFTPOS
(Electronic Funds Transfer at Point Of Sale) and EDI (Electronic
Data Interchange). These systems can be generally in use (such as
EFTPOS) or written for a specific business's needs (the stock
control system at a large retailer, for instance).

When all the technology comes together...

If you are not a major supermarket or retailer, you will be more
interested in the other strands of new technology. These all rely on
a sophisticated system of satellites orbiting the planet and are,
essentially, methods of communication. There are three main
elements:

- the Internet and the World Wide Web
- mobile telephones
- digital music, television and the 'information age'.

The Internet

The Internet started out in the 1970s as a way for defence chiefs to pass information from one computer to another in order to preserve it in times of war or crisis. Data was beginning to be stored electronically and needed to be kept safe. Panic about the 'red threat' (the USSR or China, take your pick) gave the armed forces cause to worry about losing electronic information like missile codes. It did away with the need for central communications networks and storage by allowing computers to pass information (usually in the form of text) to other computers. The idea was that if one command post was knocked out, other posts could still access the information. The original network was called Arpanet and belonged to the Pentagon.

Happily, universities saw the potential for sharing knowledge and research information and the focus of the net changed radically from defence to an interactive, information-based resource. Computer languages were then developed which allowed almost anyone to write data which could be read by many systems. Browsers – the clever devices that allow you to 'surf' – followed, most notably Netscape Navigator and, later, Microsoft Explorer. This meant that anyone could now use the system – it was no longer limited to academic institutions and the Pentagon. The potential of the Internet is its greatest attraction; there is no way that even a tenth of its potential has yet been harnessed. What it allows you to do at the moment – buy a book, book a flight, listen to a concert, manage your bank account, watch a movie – is nothing to what will be possible once all the new technologies are working in harmony.

Within the Internet there are a number of functions, all of which can be useful to businesses. The advantages of e-mail, for example, are obvious. Messages can be sent around the world instantly and cheaply, not just in the form of text but also pictures, scans, video and spreadsheets etc. Using service providers such as **net2phone** can bring the cost of international calls tumbling (and the quality is pretty good now) while chatrooms and newsgroups can be used to gather information and opinions. Chat rooms are areas where people can 'meet' and 'talk' to each other by typing messages in. Newsgroups are where you can place a message or question and other users can respond. Video conferencing can also take place via the Internet, which can be used as a kind of video phone by combining a web cam with a telephone link. Think about how any of these aspects could be used to enhance your business – even if they are not immediately useful for sales, they can be strong contenders for an easy and cheap way to research a particular market. Businesses should not be saying, 'These are of no use to me'. It is not just a question of asking 'How can I make use of these?', but 'How can I not only make use of these but maximize the benefits to my business of using them?'.

World Wide Web

The World Wide Web is responsible for the 'www' at the front of each web site address. It is that part of the Internet that carries web sites – pages of information that can be posted by anyone with access to the Internet and a little 'web space'. This might be text, pictures, sound, video or even live 'web cam' broadcasts. The World Wide Web was created only in 1991 at a particle physics laboratory in Geneva. Mosaic was the name of the original crude 'browser' later to be replaced by Netscape. Mosaic did not manage to take the web onto the Internet until 1993 and it was only really in the late 1990s that business began to sit up and take notice. Since that first incursion, however, growth can only be described as phenomenal.

One of the main benefits of the web is that the medium is open to anyone; one of its main drawbacks is that there is little control over the nature of the information that is posted. Thus amongst helpful, amusing, educational and interesting sites you will also find nestled pornography, racism and other extreme views. All of these web pages and web sites are interconnected by hyper-links – words, bars or buttons which, when clicked on, take you directly to another site. The interconnectedness of all the elements make the term 'web' a particularly suitable one.

Your e-commerce web site will be part of the world wide web and will be competing for attention with all the other 'pages' of information and entertainment up there. That's why it's got to be special!

Mobile phones

Mobile phone technology leaped forward in the first few months of the new millennium. Not only are phones smaller and cheaper to buy, but many now come equipped with the ability to send and receive e-mail or to access a special section of the web through WAP (Wireless Application Protocol). WAP phones access specially designed small web pages, but have not proven to be nearly as popular as manufacturers had hoped. The content is not really available and the information which could be displayed on a mobile phone screen is limited.

WAP phones were the technology of the future, allowing some web access from a mobile phone, but, as with many other recent innovations, they are set to become nothing more than a stepping stone to the next technology. Third generation mobiles (or 3G, as it is becoming known) will combine all the best elements of current technology: web connectivity (the move is towards permanent connection to the web for a flat fee, so that there is no need to dial up); a proper, colour screen which can carry quality digital images; e-mail, text messaging and voice transmission capabilities and game player, all in the same hand-held device. As a 'half-way house' to full digital services, manufacturers have introduced 2.5G. This is based on something called the General Packet Radio Service (GPRS) which sends information in packets – faster than conventionally but not as fast as will eventually be possible. For e-commerce businesses, the important thing is that it will be permanently connected to the net and likely to include a facility for taking customer payments.

Other hardware

Computers come in a bewildering array of sizes and specifications. The biggest, and most common, is called the desktop computer. Usually this has a 15-, 17- or 19-inch screen (measured from corner to corner, as with all video and television type screens). The next size down is the laptop, a portable machine which folds flat for easy carriage and storage, usually about the size of a pad of A4 paper. This can be compatible with a desktop so that information can be exchanged between the two. A laptop with the appropriate facility is able to access the Internet via a mobile telephone connection. Laptops are getting more and more and lightweight, and screens are becoming larger and sharper. The smallest type is known as a PDA, or Personal Digital Accessory. To distinguish this from desktop and laptop it is sometimes referred to as a palm top, although this is close to certain trade names. A PDA is a hand-held device that will fit into a pocket and is approximately half the size of a paperback book. Again, this can talk directly to its laptop or desktop brethren in order to share and back up information. Other elements of technology that you will find increasingly essential are writeable CDs and DVDs (soon also to be writeable). These extend data storage capacity tremendously. Other strands of hardware development which are being brought online (and which will soon be commonplace in new systems) include fibre optics and wireless connections (wireless mice are already available as are PDAs with infra red links to their big brothers).

Digitalization

Both sound and pictures can be transmitted more quickly and with greater clarity by digital means. This has already revolutionized the quality of television transmissions and made communications much faster. The information age has moved from information delivery by analogue signal to that by digital signal – a faster and more efficient alternative. The 'digital age' is a soubriquet which is increasingly being used to replace the 'analogue age' as the defining characteristic of the new millennium. What it does mean is that more complex information – such as pictures, sound files and video – which up to now has taken an age to deliver, will be much more easily downloaded. Eventually, it means that it will be possible to use large files such as these, which take up a lot of memory, with much more confidence that web site users will be able to cope with them. At the moment, digital applications are not particularly widespread and the use of, for example, animations on a site needs to be curtailed if the site is not going to take an age to load. It is important that your site tries to cater for both old and new technologies, often this is achieved by providing a hyper-link to the relevant software for those systems that do not have it.

Bandwidth

The speed by which information can be transferred electronically is affected by the bandwidth of the communications device. A narrow band carries less information than a broad band. Broadband technology will allow more information to be downloaded and at much faster speeds. At present, the download speed is limited by the slowest part of the system. This may be a 56K modem used to connect the computer to the Internet, or the capacity of the telephone line, or the speed at which the provider can actually send the information. In the future, broadband technology, coupled with permanent, low-priced connection through special lines, will make using the Internet even easier. Speed of communication is one factor which is currently increasing rapidly. The slowest speeds are 56K (although 28K and even 14K modems may still be around); faster than this are ISDN and ASDL (see Glossary) both of which provide an 'always-on' rather than a dial-up connection. Faster still are direct cable links – it is along such links that cable companies will be able to provide television and telephone services as well as Internet connections. Another system being developed is CDMA (Code Division Multiple Access), an advanced mobile phone technology that will enable telecommunications subscribers to be provided with better quality, more sophisticated mobile services. This will lead into the next generation of mobile services. This third generation (3G) mobile technology will be able to provide a collection of services such as e-mail and Internet access, hi-fi audio, file transfer, video and interactive entertainment across a telephone network. Visit **www.telecom.co.nz** (who are developing it in New Zealand) for more details of where and when this service will be available. Professional systems may be even faster – it is inevitable that the speed of data transfer will rapidly increase.

Communications media and business transactions

The selling of goods and services to a customer via the medium of the Internet is just one of many ways of utilizing the Internet. It is worth considering whether any of the following ways in which the Internet has grown can be made useful in enhancing your own e-commerce venture. The Internet can be used as a pure communications medium or for transactions. Communications include information exchange, contact services and education. Business transactions include banking, insurance, gambling and online trading.

The information superhighway

This is a term with which most people are already familiar. It was coined to give an instant impression of the sheer volume of information that is carried on the Internet. The Internet has been described as a giant, unindexed library of the world. You can find information on any subject that interests you, or provide information yourself. It is worth remembering that most of the information has not been vetted for accuracy or validity – some sites post information that is untrue or biased (often in order to support a particular viewpoint) so it pays to be aware of the source of certain information.

The key for a commercial operation is how to make money out of the service. The sort of information carried might be related to one of the areas above – such as personal information, share dealing or online newspapers – or any one of a number of other different areas ranging from route maps, travel directions and holiday information, to gardening tips and advice. For example, try **www.multimap.com** for maps of the UK and Europe, for finding any location from a postcode and for travel directions; try

www.guernseytourist.com for information about this particular holiday destination (this is just an example, there are thousands more to choose from); try **www.gardenersworld.com** for gardening news, tips and advice. The information on most of these sites is free – it is the presence of either sponsorship (*Gardeners World* is a BBC television programme) or advertising which supports the site.

Contact and communications

An enormous growth area, encompassing much more than e-mail. It is now possible for the smallest of businesses (or an individual) to have a web site. A site can, for instance, be used to keep in contact with friends and family around the world or just to support a particular point of view. A site doesn't have to be trying to sell anything but can be devoted to providing or exchanging information. There are online versions of all the major newspapers and many magazines as well as some magazines that have no print equivalent, that are exclusive to the Internet. The advantages of this are obvious: photographs, video clips, sound bites and text can all be combined in a way that is not possible in any other medium. The disadvantage is that there is little to stop anyone posting any views or pictures, however extreme or one-sided. For a good example of a personal site based around a hobby or point of view (such as support for a sport) visit the site hosted by the consultant for this book at **www.ebuygum.co.nz**.

There are also many sites where people of like minds can contact each other to air views or to plan meetings, often similar to newspaper 'lonely hearts' columns. Meetings arranged in this way should be treated with great caution. The anonymity of the Internet means that people can live out fantasy lives, pretending to be what they are not. The six-foot, blue-eyed 21-year-old that you decide to meet for a date could turn out to be five-foot-three and sixty-four!

Education

There are sites that will help school and college students with homework (and less scrupulous ones that will provide ready made homework assignments), revision and study. Some educational institutions (and students) try to make money by providing essays and assignments which students can download and pass off as their own. In some cases these are even graded so that a 'D' grade student can hand in a creditable 'C' grade assignment rather than the 'A' grade one which would look highly suspicious.

University sites will both host and share research, not all of which will be available for free, and many schools also have their own (usually non-commercial) web sites. Most educational institutions are keen to provide their students with access to the Internet as a way of encouraging research and learning. Other commercial operators have based their sites around providing educational resources. One of the major UK-based sites is **www.schoolsnet.com** which carries online lessons and revision as well as details of UK schools. It also sells educational equipment and provides space for schools to advertise vacancies. The revenue from sales, advertising and the job service can be used to support the content (a pattern that can be seen in a number of successful enterprises).

As well as use as a pure communications medium, the web can be used for conducting different types of businesses, such as banking, insurance, gambling and share trading.

Banking

A number of established banks set up Internet banking facilities using passwords and, of course, bypassing the expense of buying, staffing and maintaining branch operations. In many cases this was a natural line of growth from existing telephone banking arrangements (based on the same premise of passwords for access and no branch overheads). The first UK telephone bank, First Direct (now a part of the HSBC), was also one of the first to offer online banking in the UK. Other banks and financial institutions have followed. They give the customer the benefit of instant access, of transferring money across accounts and of checking transactions. Their major (initial) drawback was the slow speed at which they could be accessed. Newer technology means that this is now much less of a problem. Online banking has thus become much more widespread as banks have convinced customers that their details, accounts and transactions are secure and have improved access speed.

Some major banks have opened up online extensions to their normal operations, whilst some newcomers have gone straight to the web to offer financial services, many gaining at least initial success as novel rivals to traditional banks. However, there has been a reaction from the customers of traditional banks who quite liked the traditional methods of operation. Planned branch closure programmes have been slowed down or curtailed – many customers prefer personal service and do not trust their details to the Internet. Some new types of branches, where customers can relax, read and drink coffee, have been trialled. This is hardly surprising when stories emerge on a regular basis of bank accounts being raided or personal details stolen from supposedly secure sites, including many major companies. The new word coined for the hacking of commercially sensitive information from companies is 'netspionage' – it is estimated that over a third of major companies have been the victims of some form of hacking, either for information or fraud. According to the Communications Management Association, a body of computer professionals set up to deal with what is being called 'cyber-crime', the problem is growing and many companies are not geared up to cope with it.

Insurance

It is now possible to insure a car, a house, a holiday or anything else via the Internet. Insurance companies (some of which are new, some of which have, as with banks, grown from telephone insurance operations) have produced online forms so that customers can fill in details and receive an instant quotation. The advantage of such a system is that quotes can easily be compared and insurance then put in place immediately. Companies should also be able to offer more competitive quotes than their offline rivals.

Gambling

Because of the international and ethereal nature of the medium, it is possible to gamble almost anywhere any time of the day or night. This has meant that bookmaking operations no longer have to be on the high street, or even in a particular country. Punters can bet on horse races that are taking place anywhere in the world or can even gamble in virtual casinos. One knock-on effect from this has been that the UK government has abandoned betting tax as it was becoming increasingly impossible to collect it.

Online share trading

Traditionally, most people could not take part in the rarefied game that was international share dealing. To buy a share you had to first contact a bank or broker, who would then buy the share on your behalf, being licensed to trade on a stock exchange. It was equally difficult to sell shares quickly – essential if you want to take a quick profit due to a share price movement. The Internet has changed all of this so that shares can now be bought and sold by anyone, online, with an immediacy that has never been possible before. This has meant that amateur speculators have been able to track the movement of their shares and to buy and sell without the delays of traditional share dealing.

Advertising

This is the method by which many businesses can afford to give away information. In many cases the information or advice is freely available and the site makes its money from carrying advertising. The theory is very similar to that of the 'free' newspaper. These newspapers are totally funded by advertising revenue and therefore carry very little news in relation to the amount of advertising that they have.

Does anyone actually read a free newspaper? Or do they just use them on those specific occasions either when they want to advertise something for sale or when they are searching for a particular bargain? Many web sites suffer from the same problem – they carry so much advertising that it is difficult to get to the 'meat' of the site. The advertisements are often in the form of banners or animations and, as such, can take a long time to download. Many will also be trying to lure surfers away from the site by actually being hyper-links to other sites.

Many e-commerce enterprises that relied almost entirely on advertising for their revenue stream have found that advertising revenues have gradually fallen and, in some cases, vanished altogether. This has happened as advertisers have found the medium to be less effective than they had hoped and cut down on the amount of advertising they were willing to pay for. Businesses that were relying on advertising to 'keep them afloat' whilst they built up the 'real' side of their business have often been plunged into difficulties. Over-reliance on advertising revenue combined with slower than anticipated growth of sales has been the cause of a number of Internet business failures. Some commentators, however, insist that advertising is the necessary evil that allows the Internet to continue to grow.

Entertainment

Apart from selling entertainment such as games, videos, DVDs and CDs, the Internet provides a medium through which other entertainment can be provided. Some material can be downloaded for free while other material is subject to a subscription or membership charge. Napster led the way in providing a 'music swap' site where people could download music for free, and, although this is still the subject of legal wrangling, it has had the effect of making the big music companies provide their own online services. There are also sites where games can be obtained or played, or where 'cheats' for games can be found. Along with these are personal sites which have little purpose other than to share the host's sense of humour with others – sites with jokes, anecdotes, riddles and other humorous (sometimes) devices, posted with no intention of making any sort of commercial gain.

The future

The future is developing extremely rapidly. While this book has been written with the intention of being as up to date as possible, it is inevitable that new systems will be in place before long. The buzz words of B2C, B2G and B2B are unlikely to be replaced with new ones as such transactions will still be taking place, but may be joined by new coinages. (Currently doing the rounds is E2E, Exchange to Exchange, where one market place joins with another and connections between major players worldwide can be forged. For example, General Motors and Ford have created a huge electronic market place to source and price components.) The technology is rapidly developing so that what was new only a short time ago is quickly superseded.

? Did you know?

Information technology exhibitions tend to showcase new technology that is in development or about to hit the markets. In 2000 it was WAP phones, in 2001 it included a wristwatch-sized phone and messager, a cordless Internet radio and a digital camera application that attaches to a mobile phone and allows images to be sent to other, similarly enabled, phones or computers. By 2005 it is likely that they will be showcasing combined video camera Internet-enabled mobile phones which have the facility to transfer credit (so that you can pay for purchases), perhaps with iris recognition built in for security. All (as James Bond has demonstrated in the past) are possible, and it is likely that they will all be matched together at some point. Technology, at present, appears to be limited only by the bounds of imagination.

! Hints and tips!

Make sure that you take advantage of as many of the sources of free help that are available. This ranges from government advice and information to the sort of free information available from local business and trade organizations. Remember that, while you should make a point of listening to whatever advice is given, you don't actually have to act on any of it.

Web links

For examples cited in this chapter, go to: **www.multimap.com** for maps of the UK and Europe, location finding and directions; **www.guernseytourist.com** for information about this particular holiday destination; **www.gardenersworld.com** for gardening news, tips and advice; **www.ebuygum.co.nz** for an example of a personal site devoted to a hobby (or obsession!); **www.schoolsnet.com** which carries online lessons and revision as well as details of UK schools.

Also, visit **net2phone** which connects one telephone to another via a computer and modem link – ridiculously cheap!

Glossary

Business

globalization   or global markets; the increasing trend for businesses to operate with little or no regard for national and international boundaries; businesses can produce where labour is cheap, operate from countries whose laws favour them and declare profits in low tax areas

hacking   illegally entering a computer system

netspionage   hacking into a system in order to obtain sensitive or secret commercial information

SMEs   small- and medium-sized enterprises; defined in the UK as businesses with fewer than 250 employees

Information Technology

information superhighway   the term used to describe the amount of information available on the Internet

hardware and software   both essential to the operation of a computer system; the 'layered model' (see Figure 3 over page), shows the levels in a system

peripherals   'add-ons' that make a system better or more efficient, such as printers and scanners

chatrooms   places on the Internet where people can post messages and receive instant replies from other people logged on to the site

newsgroups   places on the Internet where people can post information, request information and spark discussions; often these are specific to a particular hobby, interest or group of people and are governed by quite strict rules; some chatrooms and newsgroups are 'moderated' – someone checks the content – but many are not

Figure 3 Layered model

software	user interface
database	store
network	} communications
operating system	
hardware	physical components

Summary

- The Internet and the technology associated with it is growing at a phenomenal pace; it is important to try to keep up with developments.
- Selling a good over the Internet is just one way in which businesses may trade. Banking, insurance, gambling, share trading, entertainment, education and other features can all be used for commercial gain.
- The Internet is a vast repository of information, much of it free, and not all of it accurate or true.
- Advertising revenues are used to support the free information carried on many sites.
- If introducing new e-commerce systems it is wise to let change take place gradually, otherwise you run the risk of alienating your 'traditional' customer base.
- New technology will allow easier, quicker and cheaper access to the Internet; this will include third generation (3G) mobile phone networks.
- New security systems will allow purchases and payments over the Internet to be made with much greater speed, confidence and security.

4 | WHAT CAN E-COMMERCE DO FOR ME?

'We don't need one of those, the typewriter is still doing a fine job.'

Perhaps the question might be better phrased as, 'What will happen to me if I don't embrace e-commerce?' Whilst you won't lose customers overnight, or immediately collapse in a heap of debt, the answer is that, eventually, you are likely to be left behind. Other businesses that are in competition with yours will be moving forward, whilst you stand still. You may be in a business where the notion of standing still is not a particular problem. It may, for example, be a business with an established reputation and way of doing things, a business where stability and personal contact is important. Nevertheless, if your competitors continue to move forward and you continue to stand still, then it is inevitable that you will either lose customers to them or have to watch while they gain customers that could have been yours because they provide an enhanced service.

The diagram below shows just a few of the ways in which the seven core business areas can benefit from the various strands of technology. These are just examples – there are many others. You should look at your own operations and see exactly where each could benefit from the use of new technology such as mobile communications, electronic data interchange (EDI), the World Wide Web or other advances.

Figure 4

	WWW	e-mail	EDI	new technology
Finance	• taking payments	• obtaining quotes • global shopping around	• financial transactions	• secure transactions • customer trust
Human resources	• recruitment • training	• collecting CVs and applications • team-building	• records and payments	• remote working
Customer service	• customer profiling • customer feedback	• contacting customers nationally and internationally • specific customer responses	• detailed information exchange	• keeping customer records
Production and operations	• using suppliers worldwide • customerization	• document exchange	• stock control	• team-building • group working • instant responses
Administration	• e-publishing	• sending information internally and externally • messaging	• order processing	• CD-ROM storage • Tele-working
Research and design	• researching methods and materials	• collaboration and discussion worldwide	• project management	• video conferencing • group working • instant responses
Sales and marketing	• accurate targeting of markets • entering global markets • worldwide market research	• collecting feedback	• sales processing • transactions	• e-catalogues • online presentations • sales force contactability

The key thing about e-commerce and existing businesses is that it provides an extra means of marketing or sales, whilst taking nothing away from the existing nature of the business. It is an additional benefit, obtainable for a reasonably low outlay, not a way of doing business that has to replace what you already do well. The mistake is to think that the traditional part (and character) of your business would not be able to survive if you had an e-commerce element to your business. It will not only survive, but be enhanced by the e-commerce element.

Even as a new business, you have the opportunity to set up quite cheaply (it can be much less expensive to set up a 'virtual' business than a 'real' one) and to try out your products or ideas on potential customers. Take no notice of the dot.com failures – who suffered from an excess of marketing and advertising expenditure combined with over-high expectations – and start off quietly and small.

What e-commerce offers your business is the chance to compete with competitor businesses regardless of their size and influence. Your web site fits onto the same size screen as that of the Coca-Cola Corporation or Esso. Whatever extra resources such companies can throw at their e-commerce arms, you have the opportunity to compete – in this medium at least – on a playing field that is virtually level. E-commerce offers you the chance to expand your customer base by introducing them to new products or services, by 'selling up' to them – adding value to enhance their dealings with your business. Not only can you introduce new lines, you can also use your web site for market research – asking for opinions, test marketing, trialling – at a fraction of the normal cost and with a much faster response time.

E-commerce can also take over some of the jobs which you or your staff do – payments, deliveries and even enquiries can be dealt with – leaving you free to develop your business creatively. And of course you can tap into the ever-expanding global market place.

Growth in global markets

More than ten million new users, on average, connect to the Internet every month. This sort of growth is likely to continue until virtually everyone in the world has Internet access, creating a truly global market which will amount to a staggering size of 200 million-plus people. Penetration in some countries is already reaching over 50 per cent, while others are not far behind. A further expansion is predicted to take place once access to the Internet no longer relies on a personal computer. Once the Internet is available through television (via a cable or satellite connection), manufacturers predict a further explosion of users. What will you need in order to be able to reach this vast market?

What equipment do I need?

As a minimum for good connection, speed and storage, you will need the following. (This is in Summer 2001; better systems may by now be available for the same or a lower price – for example, a new version of Windows, based on the Windows NT operating system, is due out at the end of 2001.)

Computer

Go for a reliable and well-known manufacturer so that, if there is any problem, you are working with a company with a good reputation and back-up support. Whilst it may seem attractive to have a cheap machine 'built' by a local shop, you may find either that they are not there when you return with a problem, or that they are not interested in solving your problems – their main aim being to sell you the machine. Having decided on a brand name, you do not, however, have to buy through a high street retailer. Remember, their prices include your share of their overheads, staffing, advertising etc. You are going to be a web trader, so trade over the web! With access to the Internet (via a friend or an Internet café, for example), you can buy on line. Of course, you should visit the retailer and take any free advice that they have to offer before making your final purchase. It is easy to be fooled into thinking that you are getting a good deal by buying a 'package' which offers 'everything you could possibly need', often including a scanner, a printer, even a camera. Look at exactly what is on offer before you succumb to the advertising. Often, these packages are not as good as they seem and include a great deal of software which you will not need. It is the performance specifications that are important; these are often buried amongst the 'extras' in a package.

Speed and size

You need first to decide whether you want a desktop or a laptop. Laptops are more portable and just as versatile, but are also more expensive and more likely to be stolen. The advantage of being able to take your work with you wherever you go has to be weighed against these security risks. Desktops can take up an inordinate amount of space, but, for most businesses, desktop machines are the preferred option. Your brain can hold information, process information and remember information. The larger your memory, the more you will know, but whether or not you can use your knowledge depends on the speed at which you can access the stored information and the efficiency with which you can process new information. So it is with a computer. Your system has a speed at which it operates or processes (the speed at which it can 'think'). This is governed by the efficiency of the 'chip' which operates it, its memory or stored information, both on the hard disk and held in its RAM or Random Access Memory, and the efficiency of its operating system.

The most widely used operating system is Microsoft Windows, of which there are various versions, the latest being Windows ME (the millennium edition). Beware, later versions of some software do not have compatibility with earlier versions built in. For example, Windows '95 users cannot read files saved in Windows 2000. While it is slower, less efficient and more likely to stall or collapse than its rival Mac system, Windows is still the industry standard. Buying a Macintosh is likely to make you the darling of the publishing world, open up excellent photo and video editing facilities and show that you have a certain style; buying a PC is (unfortunately) likely to show that you have more commercial sense. Try to avoid 'pre-installed' versions where you don't actually purchase the CD. If anything goes wrong, this means that you can't fix it yourself.

The 'motor' of your system is the chip. You need one that runs at 700 Mhz or above (the higher, the faster, the more expensive), from a recognized manufacturer such as Pentium. You need at least 128 megabytes of RAM (with good Level 2 cache memory – this improves its efficiency), a spare memory slot so that you can expand the machine if you need to, a sound card (probably from SoundBlaster) and a graphics card. These may seem obvious, but are not always included.

Drives

Software has to be loaded on the machine and information saved. To do this you will need various drives. The size of the hard drive governs the amount of information that your computer can actually hold. A few years ago, a one-gigabyte drive would have seemed large, now ten-plus gigabytes for a hard drive is common. A CD drive is standard, and CD/RW drives allow you to 'burn' information on to a blank CD (the RW means Re-Writeable). You may also want a DVD drive in order to be able to load and watch movies. There are combined CD/RW and DVD drives on sale. Even with the new technology, you will still need the 'old' 3.5-inch floppy drive. You will also, of course, need a modem. This can be internal (the usual offer from a retailer) or external. An external modem has the disadvantage of extra wires and connections but the advantage of being accessible should anything go wrong. Finally, go for a good, fast printer, a scanner and a 17-inch screen. The extra size will make working on the computer so much easier.

To see what is available and what it will cost, visit a manufacturer's site like **Dell.com** where you can add to or take away from a standard system and see the price automatically adjusted.

Getting connected

As a business, you need to ask whether you need a second phone line. Most of what you do via your web site can be done offline so, at least initially, there will be no need for a second line. However, particularly if you are working from home, it is a good idea to have a second business line installed so that you can more easily divide 'home' from 'business'. If you are working from a business premises, you may not want to have a second line installed until you know how successful your e-commerce venture is going to be.

For the time being, you can use your mobile line as a back up. Every business (almost without exception) will now have access to a mobile phone so you should make sure that this number is prominent on stationery and advertisements as well as your usual number. It is only at the point when either you begin to lose customers because they are unable to contact you or you find that your site is successful that you will need a second line. Remember, you don't have to be online to alter the web site, to compose e-mail, to read e-mail, or to process orders. You can log on for a short period to send or receive e-mail or make changes, then do everything else offline. Of course, some deals may include an ISDN or broadband connection which means that you are permanently connected to the Internet for a set flat fee. In this case you really will need a line to make and receive your normal phone calls. Many businesses already have a second line for the fax; this can be 'split' with a double connector so that it is faxes that are held up whilst you are on line rather than phone calls. For an 'always on' alternative that will manage both Internet access and telephone calls (and often other services as well) you should find out if your area is eligible for ADSL or cable connection. ADSL uses most of its capacity to downstream to you and only a small part to carry messages out. Thus it can transmit at high bandwidths on existing phone lines. Cable provides even more bandwidth and therefore even faster connection. You may need to 'grow into' these alternatives as your e-commerce business grows.

You will also need an ISP (an Internet Service Provider) and web space. The minimum you should expect is five megabytes of web space (you may prefer to go for an ISP which provides more) plus an e-mail account with five or more e-mail addresses. More details are included in Chapter 10. If you are going to set up a web site then you will also need your own domain name. This means that instead of something not particularly memorable, such as **www.sites.serviceprovider.net/yourbusinessname/homepage** (for your buiness name online) you instead use **yourbusinessnameonline.com** (see Chapter 10).

Even getting online has changed. Browsers are virtually self-installing from CD or similar devices; upgrades and solutions are then available over the net. The device that connects the computer to others via a telephone line – the modem – has become faster and the amount and speed of information exchange will be much enhanced when broadband technology is generally available. The speed of change means that this may have happened before you read this!

That you are reading this book in English means that you have a good command of the language. This gives you a head start as the most widely used language on the Internet is English. The majority of the huge worldwide market will trade in English, even if it isn't their first language and will fall into – as far as you are concerned – two distinct categories. These will either be potential customers for your business, or other businesses which may either be competing with you or could be of use to you as, for example, a supplier or partner. You will need to know what each type is doing.

Potential customers

Many of the potential customers, individual users, will only ever use the Internet for e-mail. This is the most common and widespread use and, even though they are connected to the Internet, many will never think of using any of its other functions or areas. Others will surf for specific information only and may not be interested in buying; a school student, for example, may look up information for a project or investigate an area of interest such as a sports team or band. Many will not have the 'technology' to purchase over the Internet as they will not be old enough to hold a credit card. Indeed, there is a potential market of several million teenagers in the UK alone that e-commerce providers are unable to tap into. (One scheme is for teenagers to be able to hold a card which is 'loaded' with cash, so that they can buy over the Internet.) Some people will be more interested in newsgroups and chat rooms (the big attraction is that you can pretend to be someone else) than in commercial sites, others will just be interested in playing games or obtaining free music files. You will need to consider how each of these potential customers can actually be accessed by your business. Some suggestions are given in later chapters.

Others will grasp the potential of the Internet with both hands. They will conduct their banking business, download music files, gamble, deal in stocks and shares, investigate, book and pay for holidays and watch jerky and disjointed broadcasts of live rock concerts (at least until broadband technology catches up).

Some – by no means a majority even of this group – might actually buy something from the net. Many will be put off by the fear of putting personal or sensitive information onto the Internet and having it copied or stolen. Many people are quite happy to give a credit or debit card number over the telephone (not as secure as you may think) but are scared to give the same information to the Internet. Not surprising when you see the number of reports of card fraud via the Internet. Later chapters show how you can reduce the element of risk for your customers – but you've still got to get them on board first. Others will be just the sort of people that you are looking for – those who are wanting to shop over the Internet, who have the requisite credit cards and who are keen to spend money. You still need to attract them to your site, to spend money with your business.

How will they find me?

If there are two hundred million Internet users (and rising) and I have just one web site, does this mean two hundred million visitors and me not able to cope with them? Or does it mean that finding me is like searching for the proverbial needle in the haystack? It is the size of the resource itself which daunts many small businesses. 'How will anyone ever find us?' is the question at one end of the spectrum – the pessimistic end; 'How will we cope with a million orders from a hundred different countries?' is the equally desperate plea from the optimistic end.

For the first, there is an entire industry devoted to bringing order out of the chaos. Search engines, meta search engines, portals for specific information and ISPs with their own web content are all there to help and, amazingly, are usually free. These are explored in Chapter 10. For the second, while it is always possible that your site will get a few million hits, it is not very likely. And while you obviously want as many hits as possible, you also want to be able to cope. A concerted 'attack' on a web site – when as many hits as possible are made in a short space of time (sometimes called 'flaming' a site) – can crash the site and has been used as a form of demonstration against certain corporations. As long as you don't offend any powerful groups, this should not happen to you!

'No, it's *this* coach that I've got to get into, I'm just not sure why!'

Head first into the deep end

The first thought of many a business, new or established, is that, 'If you're not in it, you can't benefit from it'. Of course this is true. Businesses – rightly worried about missing out on new markets and opportunities – have dashed for the net, got themselves on it, and only then stopped to think what they are doing and how best to take advantage of the new technology.

The biggest mistake of such businesses has been to make the assumption that having a web site would be enough – that merely by establishing a presence on the web, customers would naturally follow. What is important, and what businesses should have learned from the first round of Internet successes and failures, is to have the right strategy for your business in place. You do need to accept that a strategy of ignoring the Internet is not a sound one, and to develop an appropriate e-commerce strategy for your business.

Other businesses

Other businesses may be direct competitors for your particular product, service, innovation or idea. They could be huge corporations or tiny one-person operations (there is no real way of knowing by just looking at a web site). They are all reaching the same multi-million audience as you are. Even if they are not competing directly, they are certainly competing indirectly for the time and attention of net users.

Firms could be competing directly for your business – in which case you will need to know exactly what they have on offer and how well they present it. Are they local, national or international. Are they using the Internet for advertising and marketing or for sales? How does their e-commerce operation add value for their customers? All this information can help you to make your site even better and more effective.

You could also look at their relationship with your own particular supply chain. Are they likely to be in competition for suppliers of raw materials or components, or for service providers? It may be that it is of mutual benefit for you to link up with a potential competitor as a partner. Strategic partnerships (see Chapter 14) can be built to help enhance both your business and theirs with no detriment to either.

Cost

And the cost? There are now many 'free' Internet service providers. Free in the sense that they do not charge you for the amount of time that you spend online; free in the sense that they are provided free on CD. Some will also provide you with free web space. The most innovative of these, breaking the mould of the 'pay' servers, was Freeserve, developed by the Dixons group. Users still had to pay, however, for the time that they spent online, usually costed as a local rate phone call. This could make use of the Internet prohibitively expensive to businesses, who would mostly be using the Internet during business hours at peak rates. It could also reduce the responsiveness of the business to customer needs if its one phone line were to be permanently engaged. In America, who are further ahead in some respects (not all – the American use of mobile phones, for example, lags behind its European counterparts) local calls are free so access to the Internet has never meant having to run up a huge phone bill. In the UK the pendulum has swung from the possibility of completely free and unfettered Internet access to a probable system of paid-for but unmetered access. Developments, in this as in everything else, are permanently ongoing. You may also have to pay for, depending on the options that you take, web site design, web site hosting, page storage on a server, secure transactions and web site maintenance. All of these can be either in-house or bought in and costs for none of them are excessive.

Trusting the staff

Many small enterprises (and others) are already online but few are yet taking real advantage of the potential that this opens up. You may fall into one of the following categories and will need to take the appropriate corrective action:

- **Micro businesses**. These are businesses with ten or fewer employees. These are often connected to but make little use of the Internet. Many employers are afraid of where their employees will go or what they will get up to. They are afraid that staff will use access for time wasting rather than information gathering. Usage of e-mail only is restricted to a limited number of staff – and then only if the owner can see an immediate benefit from this. You need to trust your staff – not everyone wants to surf pornography sites all day – and the benefits will begin to flow.

- **Small- and medium-sized enterprises (SMEs)**. Staff may be able to access the Internet but often the web sites of SMEs are either non-existent or poor. This can be because the business has no one who can take responsibility for a development such as a web site – a development which may be seen as not bringing enough reward to justify the investment of time and expertise. In the UK there is government help available – not least the fact that small businesses can offset the costs of technological development against profits. The government is encouraging SMEs and the aim is to have one million trading online by 2003. Use the government help, it's free!

- **Large firms**. These fare no better in the UK. In a survey of 200 large UK businesses in 2001, the accountancy firm KPMG found that 40 per cent of them (excluding specialist information technology businesses) did not allow staff to access the Internet unless they had attained some sort of management status. Again, it is a question of trust. You can limit the areas that your staff can visit or you can set up an intranet for your business (an internal web of pages).

Enhancing existing businesses

Almost any business can be improved with an e-commerce strategy, although some will gain more benefits more easily than others. If your existing business gets a good deal of enquiries and sales leads by telephone, fax or e-mail, then it will be easier to benefit. In particular, if a sale can be made by telephone, this can be adapted to selling over the Internet. If you are not a business that gets many enquiries in this way (perhaps you are a tradesman who relies on word-of-mouth recommendation, or a service provider who relies on passing trade) then it is unlikely that by merely by putting up a web site you will generate many more sales leads. What you will need to do is to attract people to your site. You will need to decide if the time and money spent promoting a site (which could be spent promoting your business) is worth it and will probably need to take a fairly long-term view. This could begin to get prohibitively expensive if it means effective advertising – putting your web address on the side of your van and on your notepaper may be cheap but is not likely to be particularly effective.

Logistics

For an existing business, the main difference between your online trading and your current trading is that you are not face to face with your customer. This gives you three logistical problems:

- How do you answer questions or enquiries?
- How do you take payment?
- How do you deliver?

Questions and enquiries

This means that your customer is therefore not able either to ask questions of you or your sales staff or to take the product away with them to test or try. Look at the nature of your business to help you decide on an appropriate e-commerce strategy. What you do already will have a large influence on what e-commerce can do for you.

If, for example, your business carries out a lot of its sales by telephone or mail order, it will be fairly easy to adapt for e-commerce. Even in these circumstances, however, customers are usually able to ask questions of the staff: How big is this? Will it fit in a standard whatever? Does it come in alternative shades, if so, what other colours does it come in? Are there other varieties? Will it go with my product which I bought from you last year? Do I need any sort of special tool with which to install it? Is it adjustable?' etc. The web site is, after all, just a means of communicating with a customer. Its problem lies in that it is only one-way communication, not the two-way exchange that a customer could have with, for example, a telephone sales representative. You will need to think of what the likely questions are going to be and answer them before they are asked. This section of your web site is usually referred to as the FAQ or Frequently Asked Questions. You should use your experience of dealing with customers to compile a list of possible questions, trying to cover all possible eventualities. You can also use this to add value to the sale by anticipating customers' requirements and having the necessary advice or product available. For example, if the FAQ is, 'Does it need a special tool to install it?' it is important that if you answer 'yes' the tool should be available, either directly from you or from a linked web site. Think of what you would do if the customer came into your business and asked the same question. You would either sell them the tool or point them in the direction of somewhere that they could buy it. This is basic communications, and no different from what may happen via your web site.

You have to make that communication as trouble free as possible by providing ways in which any transaction can easily take place. Otherwise, your existing customer will revert to tried and tested methods (such as telephone calls) and your potential new customers will be lost to you for good.

Taking payment

There are now a number of different ways in which you can safely take payment over the Internet, including the facility to take very small or 'micro' payments. Your problem will lie in persuading your customers that the transaction is safe. See Chapter 13 for more on this.

Delivery

Look at what your business is selling and compare this with what sells well over the Internet. The best thing is to sell a product where delivery can take place over the medium itself, i.e. electronically. If you are selling software, for example, this can be delivered online. Publishing online is another possibility. Think of products which have been sold via telephone or mail order – flowers, chocolates, CDs, DVDs, videos and books – and they can be easily adapted to Internet sales. Some products are not so easy to deliver – think of anything that needs to be fitted, or tried on, or tasted, or tested. For your own business you must decide what is and is not possible. A local Chinese restaurant or pizza parlour might be happy to take telephone orders when they are open for local delivery. A web site to take further orders may look like a good idea, but only if they are prepared to provide 24-hour service and deliver to anywhere in the world! More ideas for success – as provided by the American government – can be found at **www.sba.com** (SBA is the Small Business Administration) which starts with a page on 'How to be successful'.

Good practice

The enhancements which your e-commerce strategy can bring are closely allied to the benefits that your business brings its customers in the real world. Existing good practice should not be discarded but expanded to take account of the new medium. Think about how you currently do things and then at how e-commerce can improve this. For example:

- Can you take queries at any time of the day or night?

  Existing – you can use an answering machine, fax or e-mail.

  E-commerce – now you can also answer questions through your FAQ and take orders and payments.

- Can you easily contact your customers with new offers?

  Existing – you can use mailshots or traditional forms of advertising.

  E-commerce – you can encourage them to visit you (or at least your web site) for information on new deals, products, offers, etc. If successful, this can do away with much of the need for advertising.

- Can you add value to your sales?

  Existing – you can add a personal touch, advice or information, special offers, incentives to return and make future purchases.

  E-commerce – adding value is the most important element of successful sales. You must use your e-commerce facility to ensure that none of the above is lost, but that something else is gained. A special discount for ordering online, for example, or products and features that are only available, or available at an earlier date, on your web site. It is vital to strike a balance between encouraging customers to your e-commerce facilities whilst not alienating those who still want to use your 'traditional' facilities.

Old and new

Don't ever be persuaded into thinking that electronic transactions will totally replace 'real' ones. Shopping via the Internet, whilst not being anti-social, is basically an a-social exercise. Shopping in itself is often a social activity. Think of the teenage shopping trip, or of going out 'into the town' or off 'to the mall'. Think of what is involved in the ritual of shopping, most of which is lost if you shop online.

?
Did you know?

TiVo is part of the new technology revolution that is beginning to combine computer and television technology. You can pause live television programmes and expect 'intelligent' automatic recording of programmes that you might like. The latest version combines TiVo with net access and a DVD player.

!
Hints and tips!

The easiest things to sell over the web are those things that could be sold by telephone and that are easy to deliver. Best of all are those products which can be delivered via the Internet, such as software or information. For goods, a postal service will be cheaper than couriers but may not be as fast or as reliable.

Web links

For help and advice from the American government small business administration go to **www.sba.gov**

For the sales site of Dell computers go to **dell.com**

Glossary

Business

market research   finding out information about your market or potential market

test marketing   marketing a product in a restricted area first, in order to gauge consumer reaction

trialling   testing a product on a small number of people, or in a particular situation

Information Technology

performance specifications   the key features of a computer

CD/RW drives   a drive that will both read and write to CDs

RAM or Random Access Memory   memory where the computer stores information temporarily; the memory empties when the machine is switched off

flaming   when as many hits as possible are made on a web site in a short space of time in an attempt to crash it

modem   modulator/demodulator; the link between computer and telephone line

ISDN   Integrated Services Digital Network; phone line capable of transmitting higher volumes of information than standard phone lines

ADSL   Asymmetric Digital Subscriber Line; able to transmit digital information at high bandwidths

ISP   Internet Service Provider

intranet   a set of web pages accessible only from within an organization; often used in education to limit the access of pupils to particular material

Summary

- Joining the e-commerce revolution is going to be essential for the survival of many businesses.

- Your business does not have to lose any of its traditional qualities or methods – e-commerce can enhance these.

- You can use a web presence for more than just sales.

- There is a basic set of kit that you will need, if you aren't already web enabled.

- Businesses need to trust their staff with the Internet.

- There are two groups of interest to a business, potential customers and other businesses.

- Potential customers are attracted by value added more than by anything else.

- Other businesses may make useful partners rather than rivals.

- You need to know how you will solve your logistical problems of answering questions, taking payment and making deliveries.

5 | THE BUSINESS PLAN

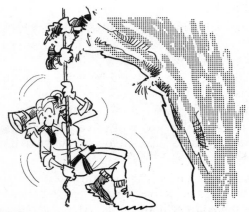

'We definitely had enough rope, it's the cliff that's obviously got higher.'

Maybe the idea of a business plan sounds a little bit too much like a case of using a traditional tool of business on a new aspect of business that doesn't need it. You would be wrong to think this. The important word is 'business' and writing a business plan is just as important for an online business as it is for any traditional business type.

You are either an existing business or you are just starting out – the business plan is just as vital in either case. If you are an existing business then you will know that your business plan needs changing and upgrading every year. As situations change or targets are reached it is necessary to revise your planning. As a business start-up you will need the plan both for your own sake and for the benefit of your financial backers. A business plan is a way to see how your new business could or might grow and succeed without taking the actual risk of investing any cash. It should include details such as cash flow forecasts, break-even forecasts and a business model. It should be based on research that you have carried out to a high and accurate standard and should include all aspects of the business, not just finance but the goods and services that you have on offer, your marketing, your structure and your administration. A good business plan lays down the direction that the business will take and delineates targets and objectives. It is used as a management tool; a tool which shows that you know what you are doing! And you are going to need to show it to the bank manager. Not necessarily because you want to borrow money, but because you will need your business account to be awarded a special status called 'merchant status' if you intend to take payment over the net using debit or credit cards. Because you are remote from the buyer you need a system that will take payment on the basis of 'Cardholder Not Present'.

Where are you now?

All business activity takes place within a certain context. Within this context business objectives are set. You then need to define the strategies (or plans) by which you intend to reach these objectives. Imagine yourself as a runner going for a five-mile training run. You have a mission, an objective and a strategy. Your 'mission' could be to keep fit, it could be to enjoy yourself or it could be to be faster than anyone else. This mission could be embodied in your 'mission statement', which would be very different depending on which of these three was your aim. Your mission statement as a business outlines your general aims and gives an idea of the context in which your business will operate. It provides the framework for your business activities and gives direction to your business planning. You can see from even this simple example that a very different training plan would be needed depending on which of the 'missions' was chosen.

Your 'objective' will be more precise and probably shorter term – to get to the end of the five miles. You may be able to set a target – one that is quantifiable or measurable – taking a particular time to cover the distance, for example, or beating a previous time.

A business will have certain objectives and short-term targets that should be fairly easy to measure. Your 'strategy' is the method you employ to reach your aim. In the case of your run, it might be a lengthy training programme, it might be harnessing your natural talent, it might be enrolling on a weight watchers course! A business will look at the possible ways to bring about the result that it wants. Your business also operates within certain parameters or constraints often laid down by legislation, sometimes just accepted good practice. These include trading laws, taxation and consumer protection issues – the last perhaps being even more important for web-based trading than for normal business transactions due to the remoteness of seller from buyer. You need to start your business plan by considering what the mission of your business is (and 'to make a profit' is neither sufficient nor smart, although it is likely to be one of your aims). The mission statement says, 'This is what we do; this is why we are in business' and should generally be customer focused.

Strategic planning

The first part of the exercise is to identify exactly where your business is now. This is often not as easy as it sounds, but there are a number of management techniques that can help you. Strategic planning involves a business asking itself a number of key questions:

- What are our aims? Where are we going?
- What is the market position of the business?
- What are the strengths and weaknesses of the business?
- How did we get to where we are?
- How will we get to where we want to be? What are our best strategies?

SWOT analysis

One tool for answering some of these questions is called SWOT analysis. This is a way of highlighting the internal strengths and weaknesses of your business and the external opportunities and threats. An internal audit of your business will show you where your particular strengths and weaknesses lie. The objective is, obviously, to build on the strengths and eliminate the weaknesses. Strengths could include your product or service itself, your own skills or dedication, the quality or experience of your staff, your financial position, your marketing talents, even the people with whom you network. As an existing business one of your main strengths will be your level of business experience. Weaknesses might be financial, or in staffing, recruiting or training. The often fatal weakness of many businesses is its lack of planning.

External factors are those that are not within your control. One external factor that you are currently taking notice of is the growth of the Internet. This highlights the fact that an external factor may be either opportunity or threat depending on how you deal with it. Treat the growth of the Internet as an opportunity and your business will grow, treat it as a threat and you could well fail because competitors have taken advantage of it. Other external factors may include government (sometimes good for business, sometimes bad for business), new firms entering your market, new methods or new consumption patterns.

SW stands for internal Strengths and Weaknesses:

- **Strengths**. This could include items such as your business reputation or brand recognition, or the customers that you currently have.
- **Weaknesses**. Could include a lack of knowledge about new technology, or not being able to trust your staff with new technology.

OT stands for external Opportunities and Threats:

- **Opportunities**. This could include new methods of production or distribution, new materials or new methods of communication over which the business has no control.
- **Threats**. This could include threats from local, national or international governments or bodies – new laws or regulations, for example.

PEST analysis

This is a way of analysing a number of external factors to see which ones are having the most effect on your business and which can be used to your advantage. The factors are Political, Economic, Social and Technological. Political factors include government at local, regional, national and (in some cases, like the European Union) supranational level. Economic factors look at the changes in consumer demand and the economic causes of those changes. Social factors look at the changes in consumer demand brought about by changes in attitudes or in society and may be considered to include changes in attitude brought about by environmental concerns. Technological factors look at changes in technology.

Objectives

Business objectives can be put into three separate categories: satisfying, maximizing and minimizing objectives. Many small- and medium-sized businesses remain in business because they have set themselves satisficing targets and succeeded in reaching them. Sometimes these targets are self-explanatory, such as, 'I will be satisfied if I am still in business at the end of twelve months'. A satisficing target is one where the business can say, 'I am satisfied with this, I am happy with this position'. It may, for example, be breaking even (see page 73) or making enough income to carry on or to finance an expansion into e-commerce.

Maximizing objectives are those where a business wants to reach the maximum – the most – of something. The most common reason given for businesses to be in business is not 'to make a profit', but 'to make as much profit as possible'. Many business theorists and commentators have made the assumption that most businesses are profit maximizers and much of traditional economic theory revolves around the 'profit maximizing' firm and the single target of getting the biggest possible gap between costs and revenues. There are, however, a number of other areas that businesses might wish to maximize. Business guru Peter Drucker suggests that there are eight possible areas in which firms may have objectives and that profit is only one of them. The other areas are linked to staff and people issues, resource issues, marketing, social responsibility and innovation.

Staff and people issues include maximizing the effectiveness of management and manpower – having managers who are efficient, well trained and loyal, and having workers who are well educated, trained, experienced and efficient. Resource issues include having reliable and cost-effective suppliers and efficient machinery and production methods. Marketing aims might involve different areas to maximize. These could be, for example, maximum market penetration, a diversity of markets or market domination. Many businesses would now see much benefit in having the maximization of social responsibility as a target and spend a lot of money to show that they are socially responsible and caring – reputation is increasingly important. Remember, for example, the enormously expensive advertising campaign taken out by one of the major oil companies whose sole objective was to show just how environmentally friendly they really were. If you are reading this book then maximizing innovation, in particular the use of new technology (although it can mean innovative products or methods just as easily), may already be one of your targets.

Minimizing objectives are the opposite to maximizing ones. The oil company mentioned above was trying to minimize the damage to its reputation caused by a run of bad publicity.

SMART targets

Objectives should be set so that they are SMART targets. SMART usually stands for targets that are Specific, Measurable, Attainable, Relevant and Time related (there are other versions with slight variations). A target should be specific – as concrete as possible – so that you can easily tell when you've reached it, measurable or quantifiable, reasonably easy to achieve, relevant to your overall business strategy and to be achieved within a certain time.

A typical SMART target for a new web operation would involve not just a hit target but what percentage of hits should be turned into sales. So it might be a target of 100 hits a week, 25 per cent of which can be turned into sales, a level to be reached by the half year. If the target is reached in advance of this, that's fine, it can be revised, but here you have a target that can be reached (attainable), is specific, can be measured, is time related and is relevant to the business. Your research will tell you what a reasonable target of this nature for a business such as yours should be.

Gap analysis

This is a fairly simple form of business analysis whereby a business can look at where it hoped to be at a particular point in time and at where it actually is. It then measures the gap between expected and actual outcome and tries to ascertain what factors could have caused the gap. For example, if the business was getting 200 hits a week but only turning 10 per cent of them into sales there are two things for managers to look at: the gap between projected and actual hits – what is causing the gap and what is being particularly effective; the gap between projected sales and actual sales – what is causing the gap and what is being particularly ineffective.

Market research

The plan can't be started without some basic research, some of which is covered in later chapters. You need, for example, to have a clear idea of which market you are targeting and why (and even of which sector of the market) and of the strength of your competition. You should also be sufficiently clued up to be able to predict the direction and development of your market. Spot a trend before it becomes one and you are on to a definite winner!

You will need to include in your plan details of market size and structure. Are you going for a mass market or a niche market? Are you looking for the whole of a particular market or a part of a much larger market? Which market segment do you intend to target?

You should also think about links between various markets. Is there anything that is likely to be habitually bought with your product and how can you take advantage of this. If you are selling handbags, for example, do women generally want shoes with them? Are you going to expand into shoes or can you link with a site which sells shoes so that you both gain benefits? This is explored more in the chapter on forging partnerships.

You can use your customers to provide a profile of your product that can be presented in the plan. Ask them for a one-word description of your product and you will get a very good idea of how customers perceive it. You can then use the descriptions to create a table which gives a good visual idea of how your product appeals to customers.

Competitors

You need to have a good knowledge of who your competitors are likely to be and in what ways they are likely to compete with you. How will their position, marketing techniques or advertising alter in the future? How will you react to change? Remember, being able to manage change is even more important for a web-based business than it is for a real one. This is explored in greater detail in Chapter 15 on people and processes.

Your research and the use of some of the analytical tools available should lead to answers to the questions posed above on page 62. This exercise in itself is a vital part of business planning and may cause you to re-evaluate your business strategy. Done properly, it can reveal a lot of information about your business and the way it operates which you might not have previously realized. Are you, for example, a business that is selling products that are at the beginning of their life cycle? Are you in a sector that is growing or declining. Perhaps most importantly, if there is information that you don't know, how are you going to find it out?

Your research can be both internal and external. You could, for example, use questionnaires with customers, suppliers and with your own staff. There are certain rules and techniques that are important if you are going to be able to use the information collected. First, you must decide in what format you would like the information before framing the questions. If you want to be able to quantify information, then an easy way to collect it is through multiple choice type answers. This is then easy to process and to present in formats such as pie charts and bar graphs. More qualitative information requires the asking of what are called 'open' questions; these elicit views and opinions and, while they can be just as valuable as the quantifiable information, are not so easily analysed. Other information available to you should include your own financial, sales and personnel figures and any information provided by consultants with whom you work. Your own business association should also be tapped for what it knows.

Action planning

Once you have answered the initial questions of where you are now, how you got there and how well equipped you are to move forward you can begin the 'action' part of your business plan – where are you going and how do you intend to get there. You should set SMART targets and outline intermediate targets (or steps) that are on the way to achieving your objectives. Details should include who is to be responsible for managing and monitoring each change, the time frame within which changes should have taken place, and what internal or external factors might come into play to help or hinder progress. It is worth outlining the best and worst case scenarios, and have strategies ready on how to deal with each. Is there a point, for example, when you would have to consider alternative options? This is not, as some commentators would claim, planning for failure. It is an essential part of the planning process. Those businesses which fail to realize their limitations, or which don't have 'escape strategies' in place, are the ones that are more likely to fail.

Presenting the plan

You should present your plan so that it looks professional and readable – otherwise it won't get read! In the following example there are ten sections – you need to cover all of the same ground but may decide on a different order of priorities. The sections here are:

- Cover
- Contents
- History and summary
- Details and legal status
- Objectives

- USP
- Market information
- Personnel
- Finances
- Any other factors of note

Remember, this is a working document for your business, one to which you and your staff can and should refer to often. You may not be intending to show it to any third party outside of the business, but its importance still warrants attention to looks and detail. To get some ideas on how your plan may be presented, you should look at the reports of a number of different companies. These are usually designed to be attractive and you can learn some tips from the way that figures are presented, or that white space is used, or on general layout issues.

Start with a cover page that contains a very brief introduction to the business. It should carry your logo and your mission statement and give an instant flavour of what your business is all about. It should be bold, simple and eye-catching. Its function is to put the reader immediately in the picture and to invite them to continue reading. It will also include some basic information about the business such as its address and other contact details.

Include a contents page so as to make navigation easier for the reader. This should have the title of each section with a one-line summary of what it contains. Again, it is basically acting as an invitation to the reader to carry on reading. It serves to give a flavour of what is in the plan and also makes it easy for the reader to jump to a particular section if that is what they want to do. Don't forget to number the pages (and yes, many people do).

A brief history of your operation – again, in order to provide a context – should be provided before moving on to a summary of the plan. This presents an overview of the plan and should include a more detailed description of the business, of the markets it already operates in and of those that it wishes to penetrate, and of its finances. This should be 'light', it should be written in as positive a style as possible but still be professional and crisp. Its function is to persuade the reader that it is going to be worth their while to read the rest of it; if it is too heavy or too detailed then many won't read any further. Use the next section to provide some details about the structure of the business. At this stage this should include the legal format of the business – do you intend to operate as a sole trader, as a partnership, as a limited liability company, as a franchise, as a co-operative? There is important information here about your intended status as regards liability. With a limited liability company (an incorporated company in America) you and the business have a separate legal identity and your financial liability is limited to the amount of money that you have invested in the company. This means that a creditor may not be guaranteed payment. Operating without this protection means that you have unlimited liability and risk all your personal assets should your business fail with debts outstanding.

Next, list your objectives and how you intend to reach them. Explain who is responsible for monitoring them and how they are to be monitored and managed. Include details of time scales for each objective and intermediate target. So, for example, you might want to say what your ultimate goal is in say, five years time and what you expect to achieve within six months, one year, two years and so on. In this section you should include any plans that you have for expansion and how you are going to cope with expanding your Internet capabilities. An Internet-based business requires good and reliable hardware and software. You need to make sure that when you expand, you have bought machinery that can cope with the expansion.

Next, compare your product with two or more competitors and justify what makes your product special. You should be emphasizing its 'USP' or Unique Selling Point. Compare features such as price, reputation, delivery and special offers. How do you add value for your customers? What is going to make them return to your site? You should include a set of basic costings for your product and show where you would expect to break even (see page 73).

Next put in your market information – the research which you have carried out – to show that your target market is vibrant and accessible. Include details of your personnel, the management structure of the business and the skills or expertise of any key staff. This should include those who you intend to hire as well as those who are already employed by you.

Finance

Your plan needs to include a section on finance. It is quite likely that you will need to raise at least some finance for your launch or expansion into e-commerce. The amount will depend on your current size and the planned speed and size of your expansion. You could be looking at fairly small amounts – maybe £2,000 to £3,000 to cover web development costs, initial advertising, buying a domain name and updating equipment (see Figure 5). A larger

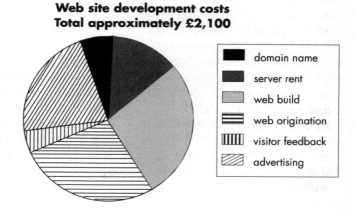

Web site development costs
Total approximately £2,100

- domain name
- server rent
- web build
- web origination
- visitor feedback
- advertising

Figure 5

business could be looking for a great deal more. There are a number of ways in which you can raise the money for either your business or, if necessary, the web part of your business. Sound business principles still apply, however – don't overstretch your resources or accept repayment terms that you can't handle. Don't accept interference in the way that you run your business either – advice, yes, but know where to draw the line. For the smaller business this will be a bank loan or the expansion could be financed from retained profits and your own funds. However, even small businesses may seek venture capital from friends, family or financial institutions. Venture capitalists lend money to enterprises, risking losing the money, in the expectation of a return. The better your business plan, the more likely you are to raise the money. A further major source of capital for bigger businesses was the city share launch; this was the main source for many 'first round' e-commerce ventures, in particular the B2C operations based on big ideas (many of which failed). **Letsbuyit.com** was based on the premise that many people coming together over the web in order to buy a particular good or service would lead to a lowering of the price – unfortunately for them, there were not enough people to immediately make the big idea work. The idea relied on large numbers of participants and so advertising was essential. This advertising had to be national and effective, meaning television, cinema and radio, which required advertising agencies, logos and brand identity, and a lot of expense. It had to be venture capital – raised through a share launch – which funded such an outlay. Venture capitalists, however, are thin on the ground now where B2C businesses are concerned. Many fund managers have specifically ruled out further investment in B2C after the spectacular collapse of so many in this sector. Instead, venture capital will be going towards businesses which have protectable new technology. This may include mobile Internet access and applications for smart cards (see Keeping it secure, Chapter 13) but is unlikely to include B2C ventures.

Finally, explain your own financial position. For an existing business you should be able to show the previous year's (or number of years) turnover, cash flow and profit and loss. You might also want to include important business ratios such as profit to sales, ROCE and acid test ratios (see page 74). If you are not an accountant it is usually better to employ one than to try to do your own accounting. Even simple profit and loss accounts can be hard to complete. For a new business, these will be financial projections and must be as accurate as possible. There are also certain accounting conventions that you would be expected to follow. Most businesses will need the services of an accountant, but you will be better served if you understand what the accountant is actually doing.

Cash flow and break-even

Cash flow and break-even are two important business techniques that should be shown in the plan. Many businesses – even big ones – fail because they have not predicted their cash flow needs. You need to predict, on a month-by-month basis, how much money will be coming into the business and how much will be paid out. This allows you to know the maximum amount of money that you will need to borrow in any period of time and should also be used to make sure that you are not 'sitting' on money that could be used for some income generating purpose. Being able to manage debt is obviously crucial, but many businesses miss the fact that it is just as important to not have too much cash in hand.

The break-even point is where your revenues equal your costs. Below the break-even point costs are greater than revenue (a loss is being made), above the break-even point, revenues exceed costs (a profit is being made). You should be able to predict how much of your product you need to sell in order to cover your costs. You should make sure that you include *all* of your costs, including your own wages and drawings, in order to give a genuine picture. You would not work for nothing for someone else, so you should include an element for the time that you spend on your web operations. To be able to calculate break-even for your web operation you will need to know what the fixed costs are – what you pay to your service provider, for example, and the costs of any new computer equipment that you have bought (spread over its predicted life time). Fixed costs for a 'real' business include the cost of premises and other outgoings such as power, rent and local taxation. If you run your web operation from an existing business premise then you should have already taken all of these costs into account and the fixed costs for web selling will be fairly small. You will also need to know your variable costs – how much does each product sale actually cost you. This includes the cost to make or acquire a physical product and the actual transaction cost. The usual method for looking at break-even is called the contribution method. This calculates how much each unit of product sold is contributing to the fixed costs of the business. It is calculated as follows:

Price minus variable costs equals contribution; fixed costs divided by contribution equals break-even. For example, if a product costs £1 to make and sells for £3, then each product sold contributes £2 to towards fixed costs. If total fixed costs are £1000 per year, then 500 products need to be sold to break even.

Ratios

The main business ratios in use are efficiency or activity ratios, which measure how efficiently you are using your resources and profitability or performance ratios. These measure the relationship between profit and other variables. The most important are liquidity ratios, which show how capable your business is of paying its debt and ROCE. ROCE stands for Return On Capital Employed and is called the primary efficiency ratio. It is calculated by dividing the capital employed by your operating profit. It is important in showing whether your business is using the money you have invested in it efficiently. You may find that you could actually earn more through a safe investment such as a bond or savings account! You will have the tools for financial calculations and predictions within most business packages – for example, a spreadsheet with graphing capabilities such as MS Excel or Lotus will be able to produce break-even charts and cash flow predictions.

Final considerations

Finally, you need to consider and plan for any other specifics in your chosen market. For example, should you have the ability to take payment in other currencies? Should you be able to take payment in new currencies (such as Euros)? Are there other variables that you need to take into account?

?

Did you know?

Business to consumer e-commerce is expected to reach global sales of almost $400 billion by 2004. Business to business (B2B) sales are expected to top this figure by at least three noughts, reaching almost $3 trillion in the same time period.

> **Hints and tips!**
>
> If you can identify a current trend and link your web operation to it you should be off to a flying start. Changes in consumption patterns can be gauged by looking at government statistics (**www.statistics.gov.uk**). For example, there is a definite trend towards more healthy lifestyles, including general fitness and healthier eating. Is there an element of your business that can take advantage of this?

> **Web links**
>
> The UK government's Office for National Statistics publishes a range of statistics, including those from the national census, and can be found at **www.statistics.gov.uk**
>
> **www.letsbuyit.com** is a web business specializing in a service of bringing buyers and sellers together.

Glossary

Business

networks, networking   often some of the most important assets of a business are the people that you talk to, those in other businesses or different fields with whom you can share experience or bounce ideas around; these are your business networks and networking can be an important tool of management

strategic planning   this involves a business asking itself a number of key questions about where it is and where it wants to be

SWOT analysis   this is a technique for highlighting the internal strengths and weaknesses of your business and the external opportunities and threats to it

PEST analysis   a way of analysing a number of external factors to see which ones are having the most effect on your business and which can be used to your advantage

SMART targets   a way of defining certain aims; SMART usually stands for targets that are Specific, Measurable, Attainable, Relevant and Time related

action planning   detailed plans which include how to reach objectives, who is responsible, when things should have happened by and what to do if they haven't

venture capital   money made available to risk on new enterprises

break-even   where your revenues equal your costs

cash flow   a prediction of the amount of money flowing into and out of a business

liquidity ratios   show how capable your business is of paying its debt

ROCE   Return On Capital Employed – important in showing whether your business is using the money you have invested in it efficiently

Information Technology

Spreadsheet   will carry out calculations and produce graphs and statistics

MS Excel   the spreadsheet that is standard on MS Windows packages

Lotus   one of the earlier spreadsheets – still good

Summary

- A business plan may be a traditional tool, but it is just as essential for a web business.
- Business plans need to be working documents, constantly updated and revised in the light of changes.
- You will need to know where you are now and where you want to be – in other words, you will need specific targets and objectives.
- There are various business tools that can be used to analyse your current position and the factors that may affect your success.

- The headings for your business plan should be: Cover, Contents, History and Summary, Details and Legal status, Objectives, USP, Market Information, Personnel, Finances, Other factors.
- You may need to raise finance – if you do, don't overstretch your resources and be careful that you still keep control of your business's direction.
- You should understand basic accounting techniques, even if you are going to get someone else to do your accounts.

6 | OPTIONS

'We won't be needing these then...'

Before embarking on any sort of web enterprise – whether it is a start-up or an expansion – think first about what you would do, ideally, if you were doing it without the benefit of the Internet. How would you carry out your proposed business? How would you attract and keep customers? Would you, for instance, be impolite to a prospective customer? Would you ignore them or respond as quickly and fully as possible? Would you offer to supply vast quantities of a product that you either haven't got or aren't sure that you can obtain? Would you break the law in the country that you are trading in? Would you refuse to accept payment if it wasn't in a currency of your choice? The basic rules of business have not changed and are not likely to. This must be a central maxim for anyone contemplating doing business on the Internet, yet you will find numerous sites where one or other of the basics is ignored or attempts are made to bypass it. This is because anyone can set up on the Internet, whereas it is usually only people with some business acumen who set up in real business!

There are a number of fairly selfish reasons why you might want to establish or expand a business – the most important (and most selfish) being to make a profit. (You may fall outside this capitalist norm and wish to provide a free service – perhaps for charity.) It is strange then that so few, even of the big name companies, actually manage to do so. Some well-known operations have still to make any money – including big boys like Amazon – while some have managed to get themselves launched (and backed by celebrities) without having actually produced anything. (Clickmango was one such site, a music site launched on the net and floated on the stock exchange, which was backed by celebrity Joanna Lumley, without having ever sold anything.) However, if you don't have a tame celebrity who is willing to front the massive advertising campaign that you have paid for, you will need a more solid business idea. In traditional business, the business produces goods or offers a service, at a particular price, and sells it to the consumer at a price which covers costs and creates a surplus, called profit. This may seem like stating the blindingly obvious, but many 'new economy' businesses seem to have failed to pick up on this central tenet.

Old and new

The Internet has divided businesses into two categories: the so-called 'old' economy, and business conducted through new technology – the 'new' economy. Whichever you feel you fall into, the best advice you can take is not to throw away the rule book. Those businesses that have tried to ignore the tried and tested methods of the 'old' economy are those that have – whether quickly or slowly – come unstuck. It should be a reassurance to successful businesses and managers that all of their hard-earned experience and expertise should not be discarded merely because they are operating through a different medium. It is essential that sensible, standard business practices be used. Keep your feet on the ground at all times! The lesson that should have been learned from spectacular dot.com rises and falls is that, if normal business practice is abandoned, normal business failure will soon follow.

The dot.com 'revolution' seemed to offer everything that the aspiring business person could possibly desire: low start-up costs, low investment and the prospect of fabulous profits. It seemed to be saying that it is possible to throw the business rule book away (indeed, some early texts on the matter actually advised just this) and that business knowledge and experience counted for little. It seemed to be promising entrepreneurs the prospect of making a fortune without taking a great deal of risk, or even putting in a great deal of effort. In fact, it seemed to be heralding a rosy business future for a much expanded small business sector.

To be successful involves thoughtful planning and making proper business decisions, based on knowledge and experience rather than on hope and speculation. As in the old economy – the 'real' business sector – you can either decide to go it alone or turn to experts for some specialist advice. The old business sector has established experts who you can turn to. They may come by word-of-mouth reputation, they may have a good history, and they may be reliable and good at their job. Because they are established you have a better chance of choosing an expert – an accountant or lawyer, for example – who is good at his or her job. In the new economy there is a lot of advice about, some of it very expensive, and not all of it is tried and tested. Remember, that one group of people that is making a substantial killing out of e-commerce is the group of web designers, consultants and Internet service providers who have sprung up in a very short space of time. You should check these out with all the care and attention that you would reserve for anyone that you were handing money to for a service. It seems strange, but while people will pay an electrician or a plumber to do a job, and be very quick to get them to return if it isn't done properly, they will end up blaming themselves for the poor job done by a 'web consultant'. They will even make excuses by saying things like 'I didn't brief him properly' or 'It's my fault, the instructions I gave obviously weren't clear enough'. There are many 'experts' out there, most of whom are self-taught (the education system hasn't had the time to catch up with the cyber-revolution yet), some of whom are extremely good and some of whom just think they are. If at all possible, use only experts who have come to you through the personal recommendation of a friend or colleague whose judgement you trust. It is also essential that you are able to see some of the work that they have completed in order to judge for yourself.

Options across the web

You may not want to use the web to sell anything; it is, after all, essentially a communications device. You may want to use it to attract people to your physical outlets, or to announce your presence without actually taking orders and payments for goods or services. Some things, as already outlined in previous chapters, do not sell well when sold remotely. For example, anything that is made to measure or needs fitting or testing is unlikely to be appropriate. Just because you are the seller of a product does not mean that you have to sell it online. This is equally true of services – if you are a cleaner of industrial boilers then you cannot sell and deliver your service over the net. You can, however, make sure that you are more visible and contactable than the next industrial boiler cleaner.

Success has generally been achieved in two ways. Firstly, through steady, organic growth rather than explosive growth, and secondly, through defining, maintaining and targeting a particular niche market (see Chapter 8). Niche markets are just small parts of a main market and, the smaller you can make your niche, the less chance there is of any competition. A niche market on the web does not, unlike niche markets in the real business world, have necessarily to be dealing in small numbers because of the ability of e-commerce to reach all the members of that niche, wherever they happen to be located.

Remember that profit, in business, is the surplus of revenue over costs. That means that you have two aims if you wish to maximize profit. One is to keep costs down; the other is to ensure that revenues are as high as possible. So how do you intend to do both of these? Keeping costs down involves managing personnel and managing waste (particularly time waste) as well as choosing reliable and competitive service providers. Revenue can be generated either through sales or by carrying advertising (your web site is, in effect, a publication, and can therefore charge to carry advertising). Many of the failed 'first round' e-commerce businesses managed to get the balance wrong. They either carried too much advertising (effectively hiding their own product and unique selling point, a bit like someone giving up watching a television programme because of the frequent and annoying interruptions of advertisements) or they tried to use advertising to make sure that their e-business would receive many visitors but then failed to deliver the goods.

Selling products

If you are in a business where you can actually sell and deliver across the net then you can learn the lessons of successful remote retailers. The most successful remote retailers are catalogue retailers and you can use their techniques when considering what to put on your site. See what information you can get from the catalogue about layout and design. See how catalogue retailers make good use of words in their brief descriptions of products. Catalogue designers are often stuck for space and must make effective use of both pictures and text. Copy what they do and you are relying on existing, successful techniques. How, for example, does the catalogue retailer answer the sort of questions that customers might ask? How do you know if this comes in your size, or colour, or the variety that you want? What sort of questions might a customer ask over a mail order telephone line and how will you answer these questions without recourse to a phone? Many web sites try to answer such queries through a FAQ section. FAQs are Frequently Asked Questions (see page 54). Such a section can create problems if the business is not really sure what the most frequently asked questions are. Look at a catalogue entry and you will see how the writer deals with such queries ('available S, M, L, XL in red, green or purple; colourfast pure cotton' succinctly tells the buyer all they need to know – this has covered the FAQs of 'Does it come in my size?', 'What colours does it come in?', 'What sort of material is it?'). You therefore need to think carefully about what information you can give to customers.

Equally, you should consider what information you can get from them – a catalogue retailer's order form or ordering telephone line will not only take orders but also take information about the customer who is making the purchase. You should, however, make sure that you only collect this information once. Think of the stages that a customer would have to go through to buy something in a retail outlet – browse, maybe ask advice, choose, pay, leave. There are slightly more in a catalogue order transaction – browse catalogue, choose, telephone, maybe ask advice, give details, arrange for payment and delivery. Your web site should have no more stages in it than this! Cut down on the amount of stages that a customer has to go through but balance this with ensuring that you collect vital information. You need to take brief details and should make the process as user-friendly as possible. Look at other web sites and see how they achieve this. In the UK, for example, it is fairly easy to link an address to a postcode database – you simply enter the postcode and up comes the address, saving your customer from having to type it in again. When they visit the site again, you should be able to trigger a response that means that only a minimum amount of information (perhaps just a name or postcode) needs to be entered for you to recognize them. This is also part of the business of 'adding value', as discussed in Chapter 1; you are recognizing a customer as an 'old friend' and can use this information to offer special service or discounts. Cookies (see 'Did you know?' box on page 92) can be used for this purpose.

Remote sales

You could actually start your Internet operation by first moving to a small mail order operation. Doing this will mean that you will learn about remote transactions and have some of the equipment and systems in place to be able to take remote orders. Start with a mail order operation and it is a natural step to move it on to the Internet. Don't try to compete in areas where it is unlikely to be possible – where established businesses got there before you and are bigger, cheaper and better organized. If you are selling the sort of goods that they also sell (say clothing, for example, or electrical equipment), then you will need to think carefully about your USP

(Unique Selling Point). What is it that will make customers come to you rather than to them? Successful Internet operations are often characterized by things that can be fairly easily packaged and delivered – books, CDs, DVDs, CD-ROMs, records, magazines and videos. (The most successful and most profitable area of the Internet is, of course, the supply and sale of pornography in these various formats, but let's assume that that is not what your own particular product is!) Can you supply something different, something which the big mail order companies don't stock, perhaps? In some cases this may be an additional service (such as personalization of an item, for example), in others it will be a particular item which is too specialist for them. Personalization is just one way of making your niche market even smaller and the word 'customerization' has been coined to combine customer with custom design. The direction of the net is towards smaller and smaller niches. The ultimate niche, of course, is the customer him or herself – a market niche of one. So can you provide designer kettles in particular colours? How about limited edition toasters? Exclusive clothes personalized for individual customers?

Niche marketing

Take a small shop selling specialist sports clothing, as an example of a combination of niche marketing and organic growth. Such a shop will be unable to compete with the 'big boys' on names such as Nike, Adidas and Reebok (each of which maintain their own web sites), or with major retailers who are able to undercut their prices, due to the volume of sales that they can put through and to restrictions placed on the supply of these items by the manufacturers. (Small shops are often put in the invidious position of having to order a great deal more stock than they need as suppliers insist that they buy in large quantities.) But you can sell more esoteric brands of running shoes (made for running rather than fashion), cross-country trainers, spikes, fell shoes and cross-trainers. Add to this your own range of socks, hats, vests, gloves, shorts and other accessories carrying your unique brand and you have sufficient range to develop a catalogue. This is usually a few pages of colour printing – not the enormous and expensive tomes produced by the big companies, and well worth the investment. Your advertising and all publicity material now mention the catalogue and it is given away to all customers. Gradually you will build up a mail order business and, if you are efficient, reliable and quick, a certain amount of customer loyalty. Hopefully, this is a similar position to the one that you are in now and this case study example comes as no surprise to you! But think about what you've done to get there. You have relied on organic growth, good service and a particular product range. Why is it that so many businesses forget all this good practice the moment that they step into the electronic world? Your catalogue can easily be put online but there is no reason to expand it massively. You don't need to spend enormous amounts of money on advertising your site either. Let customers make their way to you (as they did first to your premises and then to your catalogue) and plan for slow, organic, but reliable, growth. When you get to the right point, you may need to expand, you may need storage or warehousing facilities, you may need staff, but let the growth drive the development, not the other way around.

Audit of a current transaction

To make sure that transactions are as efficient as possible, go through a current transaction and see how much of it can be automated. First, list all the steps taken in a typical business to sell a product or service. The author's own business is called L'Avenir and sells educational consultancy services. It offers training and advice on specific areas to schools in the UK. It also designs and prepares publications and runs conferences and courses for students. In the UK there is a system of school inspections that happens to each school at least once every five years and causes mass panic at many educational establishments. L'Avenir has tapped into this as a particular niche market. The consultancy offers an affordable, one-day course in preparation for inspection which includes preparation, teamwork, and the delivery of an Alpha-plus lesson. Without the benefit of the web, this is sold through standard advertising in educational publications, leaflet deliveries to schools which are carefully targeted (schools which are about to be inspected are published on a publicly available database). The leaflet outlines information, options and prices. A follow-up phone call is made two days later to find out if the information has got through and to discover who to talk to. It is important not to lose contact at this point and to make sure that the school can contact the business if necessary. The office can be contacted 24/7 via answering machine, fax or e-mail. A preliminary visit would then be arranged. This visit is used to deliver further examples of materials used on the course and to establish rapport. In most cases a date and fee can be settled at this meeting.

The questions to ask when setting up a web-based operation are:

- What are the most expensive parts of this transaction?
- What are the most important parts of the transaction?
- How could the transaction be translated on to the web?

The most expensive parts of the transaction need to be automated or transferred on to the web. For example, the information in the leaflet and other course information can be much more comprehensively presented on the web at a fraction of the cost. There is no need for printed reproduction, or for postage. The most important part of the transaction is probably the initial contact. In the offline model this is 'cold calling' – a trader is offering services because he or she thinks that a customer might be interested. The key to the success of the Internet operation is to get the customer to contact you. This means that you are not then cold calling, you have a prospective customer who has seen and is interested in the product, and the sale is almost in the bag! Part of the transaction can therefore be transferred on to the web – the contact can be made (and is a great deal better for being made by the customer) and information can be provided. The actual course, naturally, is still delivered in the target school and payment can be made and received in the normal way. In this case there is no need or advantage for any online payments to take place (therefore no need for credit card details and password protection). In expanding the site, publications, information and course materials could be sold but the decision as to whether to do so would be made on the amount of likely sales as against the cost of setting up and maintaining safe payment options. Some businesses will be able to use a web-based shop front like Amazon and Yahoo and it is worth looking into these to see if they are useful to you (see **Amazon.co.uk**, **Amazon.com** or **Yahoo.com**).

You should carry out a similar exercise with your most common business transactions to see which can be most easily and profitably carried out via e-commerce.

Be first and best

The most successful businesses are those which have a sure-fire idea that no one has done before, that can be marketed easily and that have an immediate and huge demand. The Post-it® note or the Sony Walkman® (see Chapter 8) are obvious examples. However, should you be able to come up with a product idea that matches either of these, it is fair to say that it will sell, web or no web! If you can be first in a particular field, a particular market that no one has ventured into before, then you have a head start on the competition. Being first into the market means that you are the best (you must be, you are the only one, at least until another business is attracted by your success and comes in to compete with you. Being the first means that you will have the advantage of building up a good customer base and can perhaps build up enough of a head start to be able to discourage competition. It also, unfortunately, means that you can make all of the mistakes that others can learn from, so be careful.

It may be that, instead of a product such as those mentioned, you have lighted on an innovatory service and could set up a site to provide the service. The usual way to make money from such an operation is to charge for site membership before surfers can access the whole content of a site. Usually a few pages of information is publicly available as a 'teaser' and visitors are then asked to register and issued with a user name and password in order to gain further access. Other successful service providers include ones such as sport-related sites carrying online updates of football or other sports news and even scores; online commentaries on cricket or rugby matches, golf tournaments, tennis matches etc. (particularly popular if an international is being played abroad in a different time zone); news of events; ticket availability, prices and sales. This is where the strength of the web as a communications device will come into its own. Broadband and web-based television should mean that, in the very near future, the American will be able to watch his home town baseball game in real time from anywhere in the world, while the English person can keep up with the latest soccer news. And there is room still for the small operator, particularly in the more esoteric (and interesting) sports.

Disintermediation

This is a word that has been coined to describe the process of cutting out the middleman. E-commerce sales should mean that the seller can get in touch directly with buyers. This means, for example, delivering direct to customers from a warehouse or even from a manufacturer, and cutting out the middleman's (the retailer or wholesaler) profits. There are still many openings, however, for other types of intermediary. Many first generation Internet companies tried to cut out the middleman of a chain of supply, some successfully, others less so. Amazon has cut out the retail bookshop, but the retail bookshop (unlike Amazon) makes a profit.

There is, however, another form of middleman where there are still possible profits. This is in providing a service between two groups of people who are seeking each other.

One big area to investigate is if you can provide the link between those people who want to sell something and those who want to buy without (and this is the key thing) actually having to handle the product at all. For example, parents might be seeking second-hand prams, pushchairs or toys, other parents, whose children have outgrown them, are seeking to sell them. The traditional way for this market to be conducted would be through the small advertising columns of a local paper or (even more inefficiently) via a card placed in a newsagents or corner shop window. An intermediary type site could provide a 'market place' (an EM) where people could place items that they wish to sell and where others could visit to buy. This would be cheaper, more efficient and better for both parties – cheaper and more efficient because of the nature of the medium, better because fuller descriptions and even photographs of items could be posted. The web site owner could take a small fee for each item displayed and need do nothing more than place the items on the web and remove them once informed that they are sold.

An example for being the intermediary for a service could be the market for freelancers. The publishing and computer industry relies on freelance writers, editors, page designers, illustrators, consultants and the like. They are generally hired for a particular project and work from a home base or part time in an office and part time at home. There is an enormous supply of freelancers and a virtually constant demand. A web-based operation could accept registrations from freelancers in which they could not only describe their talents and areas of expertise, but where they could show examples of their work (illustrators could, for example, publish part of their portfolio to show style and capabilities, web consultants could provide links to successfully completed projects). A small registration fee is collected. Buyers then pay a fee to visit the site (or not, there may be enough income from the registration of freelancers) and can choose and approach the exact type of freelancer that they want.

Another option that has picked up on the idea of being an intermediary is the dating site. Again, all it requires is a number of people looking for a partner and a number of people who are willing to advertise their availability.

The key thing is that there are a number of sellers and a constant supply of buyers. The service is to stop the sellers having to look for a buyer (the buyer comes to them) and to reduce or eliminate the amount of advertising and selection that the buyer has to go through. Such a service may also be possible for those who already provide a service of bringing buyer and seller together without ever handling the product, such as estate agents. Wouldn't you like to be able, for a small fee, to put your house details on to a web site where prospective buyers will go and look? The web will allow much greater levels of sophistication than the normal leaflet distribution – for example, providing a number of photographs or virtual tours – and will also be cheaper. There is no reason why this could not run alongside the traditional estate agency, providing a wider service.

The problem with all of these intermediary type ideas is that the site has to have a high profile. If no one knows that there is a second-hand toy site, or a dating site or whatever, then they will not visit it. This often means that e-commerce ventures of this nature need a great deal of capital at the start of their business life, in order to generate the publicity. The example of **Letsbuyit.com** in the UK serves to illustrate this. Their burn rate was such that the business became unsustainable – even though the actual idea behind it was that of bringing buyers together in order to act in concert and bring prices down.

Re-intermediation

The giant Boeing Corporation of America is one of the more successful examples of re-intermediation. Where disintermediation is the buzzword that has come to mean the removal of the middleman, re-intermediation means that you replace that middleman with yourself; you become the intermediary for your own suppliers and customers. Boeing runs an electronic market place or EM in the USA. It has its own intranet or private network, as do many of its suppliers; it also has some very small and specialist suppliers who are not big enough to warrant an intranet. It also has customers. All of these are linked together in an EM where Boeing is the moderator. It maintains the links between all of its various suppliers and customers either via web links or private links. In this way, a single market place for the thousands of satellite companies and organizations which Boeing relies on is created. Boeing can monitor and control all the parts of its supply chain, from initial design through development and realization to purchasing, fitting and testing. It has an overview and a degree of control over how and when its suppliers and customers buy and sell. This gives it a power that extends much further than just purchasing power (where there are substantial gains to be made); it holds the 'strings' as it were, and has an overview that can help it in all phases of its business. This is B2B on a grand scale, but scale isn't the only consideration. Businesses can link with other businesses in simple one-on-one partnerships and gain the benefits of this sort of set up – especially useful if you link with a business that is at a different stage of your own supply chain. For example, a furniture manufacturer might link directly with a timber merchant to their mutual benefit. The manufacturer has a guaranteed supply of timber, at an advantageous price. The timber merchant has a guaranteed market for the product. It is worth looking at your own chain of supply to see where such links can be made

Be your own developer

The ability to be your own developer still depends on your having a good business idea to develop – the idea must come first. What it does mean is keeping costs to a minimum by learning to do the different jobs yourself rather than hiring in anyone to do them. You could undertake to build your own web site, carry out your own design and minimize your outlay on anything expensive that does not pay its way. Chapters 10 to 13 of this book are specifically aimed at the small business person who would like to develop his or her own web presence.

Successful Internet business

What can you learn from those businesses that have made a success of Internet trading? There are a number of points that they will have in common. Most have grown fairly slowly; they have started off with a simple site and limited products for sale. If you could see their business plans (see Chapter 5), you would see that they have planned for expansion – but a fairly steady expansion once they have established a market for themselves. Those that have tried to expand too quickly are the ones who have found it difficult. Planning for expansion should not only take account of your customers' needs and those of the market, but also of your own needs. If you are buying a new computer, for example, make sure that it can cope with everything you are likely to need over the next few years. Make sure that it has expansion slots for more memory or other cards if and when you need them. Simple things like buying a big enough case (even though it will take up more space) can cut costs when expansion is necessary. All of this should be built into your planning. Many have found a successful niche market, particularly in items that can be delivered across the web, such as files or applications. One important consideration – perhaps more so for Internet businesses than for others – is security. Your system is vulnerable to 'attack' from other users of the Internet and you can be much more open to fraud than the high street trader. Successful Internet businesses need firewalls and other security protection as outlined elsewhere in this book. Businesses have to have a certain amount of promotion so that people know that they are there and can come and spend money, but you can do too much, spend too much and be unable to recoup the outlay through sales.

Look at successful real businesses and see what sort of a balance they have struck. You won't find the corner shop or convenience store advertising on national television. You need to choose promotion that is effective and appropriate for your size and type of business. You will have a particular target market and should make that your primary concern. Certainly initially (and not until you plan to expand) you don't need to advertise or promote your site to anyone but your target market. You should also be careful that you are operating within the law – advertising should not be dishonest, or illegal, or offensive in any of the countries where you are seeking customers. Service providers may have firewalls which simply reject and dump anything that sounds offensive. (Certain towns in the UK have suffered the ignominy of having their civic web sites rejected because of certain 'words' that appear in their names!)

Another lesson that can be learned from real businesses is to react to feedback. If your customers kept telling you that your opening hours were inconvenient, or that they would like you to stock a particular product, what would you do? Similarly, your site should be set up to receive feedback from your customers, which, wherever possible, you should act on. This response to consumer feedback is one of the major benefits of the interactivity of the Internet.

? Did you know?

Cookies are tiny parcels of information that are stored on your customers' computer. They allow you to tell if the customer has visited you before, to identify them (and greet them) by name, and to point them towards information that they have not seen before. They also allow you to track how a visitor got to your site – if, for example, they came via a partner site. Some visitors may object to the use of cookies and disable the ability to receive them. Many sites will not deliver, however, if cookies are refused. You may have to convince your customers that cookies are harmless (and beneficial to the business). Your customers are not stupid and will be grateful for someone who takes the time to explain such things to them.

Hints and tips!

Successful businesses (not just Internet-based ones) recognize their own limitations and seek assistance from professionals whenever this may be necessary. Do not be afraid to go looking for help when you need it. The best and most useful help usually comes via word-of-mouth recommendation. This is much more trustworthy than just seeking assistance through the telephone directory. Make sure that you have what you want from your consultant very clearly in your mind and get them to explain what they are going to do before they do it (and don't just nod your head as if you know what they are talking about – make sure that you do understand it and ask questions if you don't).

Glossary

Business

remote sales selling that is not face-to-face – telephone, catalogue, mail order and e-commerce sales

USP Unique Selling Point – what makes your product special

disintermediation the process of cutting out the middleman

intermediation acting as the middleman

re-intermediation acting as your own middleman

Information Technology

visibility the ease with which your web site can be found

FAQ Frequently Asked Questions – the section on a web site that attempts to answer customers' queries

cookies tiny packets of information stored on a customer's computer to provide the business with feedback

customerization – custom design for individual customer's needs

EM Electronic Marketplace – a virtual market place for buying and selling

m-commerce buying and selling through mobile devices such as mobile phones or PDAs

Summary

- The rules are the same in the new economy as they are in the old economy. Sensible business practice is necessary.
- Experts can take some of the strain out of development, but they must be chosen carefully.
- Just because you sell something doesn't mean that you have to sell it on the web. It may be better for your business to use the web just as a communications device.
- If you are going to sell goods, catalogue layout can give many clues to good design.
- The Internet is a two-way street, you can collect information from your customers as well as provide them with information.
- Break down a current 'real' transaction to see how it can be transferred on to the web.
- There are a number of ways in which you can transfer your business on to the web. These include being first with an idea, carrying information services, intermediation, disintermediation and re-intermediation.
- Success often depends on your level of visibility.
- Good planning and targeting is essential.

7 | CHECKING OUT THE COMPETITION

Comparing with competitors to work out what makes yours special!

Looking at the market

If your business is involved in any of the following areas then, according to recent trends, you will find a great deal of competition on the web:

- supplying and selling tickets for entertainment and events
- travel agencies
- supplying and selling software applications
- grocery retailing
- mail order catalogue sales.

Sales of tickets across the Internet, for travel, entertainment and events, had not reached half a billion dollars by the end of 1997. By the start of 2002 this was predicted to be a figure closer to $10 billion – a twenty-fold growth in just five years. And the trend is set to continue. For travel tickets, online booking already takes more than ten per cent of the market, a figure that is rapidly rising. In entering any of these markets you may find that there is just too much competition, too well organized, for you to make much of an impression. This underlines the importance of market research, and of carving out a niche market slot for yourself only after you have seen what is already on offer. If you are supplying products or services that are outside these immediate areas, you are still likely to be faced with some competition. What you should be trying to do is to find out how much competition there is and how strong it is. Many of the techniques that you might use for finding out your offline competition can be adapted and adopted to find out about online competition. This is a vital part of your e-commerce strategy and should be a central part of your planning for success.

Competitors

Common sense and good business practice means that you ought to know what sort of competitors you have online (common sense and good business practice means that you already know what your competitors are up to offline!). Remember the maxim 'know thine enemy' and make sure that you do. This mean finding out what the competition is like in a number of areas and, at the same time, finding the areas where you might find support. Nor do you only want to know about the businesses that are competing for your custom; there may also be businesses competing for your suppliers, or for the attention of any other of your strategic partners. It is important that you take all of these into account.

Substitutes and complements

In terms of your customers, there will always be substitute products and complementary products that can help or hinder the growth of your sales. Whatever goods or service you offer, some things will be bought instead of it; these are substitute goods and services, while some will be bought to be used at the same time as it; these are complementary goods and services. Take the simple example of a fish and chip shop. Fish and chips are complements, they are bought together. The more fish that are sold, the greater the number of chips likely to be sold. This means that the demand for one has an effect on the other – a rise in the price of fish will be likely to cause a decrease in the demand for fish and a consequent decrease in the demand for chips. The more essential the complements are to each other, the more important this relationship will be. In some cases the complement may be essential for the use or enjoyment of the product. Take the example of cars – the price of rubber is directly linked to the price of tyres, the car cannot run without tyres so the price of tyres has a direct effect on the price of the car.

In our example fish and chip shop, however, fish and pies are substitutes. This means that they are products where one is likely to be bought instead of the other. The more fish that are sold, the fewer pies are likely to be bought. Again there is a relationship. If the price of fish goes up, then it is likely that at least some customers will switch their allegiance to pies instead (depending, of course, on many other factors such as taste and customer loyalty). Again, the relationship can be a very close one – the nearer the substitutes are to each other, i.e. the more similar they are, the closer will be the relationship and the bigger the reaction of the demand for one in response to a change in price of the other. Would you prefer a red cover or a black one for your diary? Personal preference will soon be over-ridden if the price of one is twice that of the other, while in all other respects they are identical!

Complements

Complementary goods can be a great help to you in your own marketing. If you know of a price change that is likely to happen for a complement, you may be able to devise a tactic so that your demand is not too badly affected. Keep an eye on sites selling complementary goods to see which ones you may be able to make a partnership with. It could be that a link between your site and that of a complementary good could prove profitable for both of you. Perhaps a specialist tool is needed in order to fit some of the parts

that you stock? Ideally, of course, you should stock the tool
yourself and offer it for sale as part of the package that you are
presenting to your customers. However, if for any reason this is not
possible, you could provide a hyper-link to a site that does provide
the tool. A sale for you is thus a sale for them also. You would
expect them to reciprocate by pointing people towards your site.
The thing to be careful of is that you are not eating into your own
market segment, this is why it is so important to define tightly the
niche market that you are targeting. Partners of this nature are
likely to be in the same business as you and could well be
competing with you. An ideal situation is where each specializes in
a different part of the same market – for example, you sell bulbs for
tulips and narcissi, and your partner sells bedding plants. You are in
the same business, you are even in the same sector of the same
business, but you are not competing directly. You could also both
link, for example, with sites selling gardening implements or
garden design services.

Substitutes

Substitute goods are a different concern. You should categorize all
substitutes according to how closely they match your product. Are
they perfect substitutes or a long way from being this? Perfect
substitutes are products that are exactly the same as yours – you
may even share a supplier with competitors meaning that both
products and costs are likely to be identical (see below). Close
substitutes are those which share some features with yours but
where there are differences. There will also be distant substitutes –
look at these and see if you think that they are distant enough to not
affect your market. You should list substitutes and then give each a
number: one for a perfect substitute down to ten for a distant
substitute. You can then enter this information into a table, where
the third column contains the details of the competitor businesses
which you have found out from your offline and online searches
(see page 180). In this way you will very quickly get a good idea as
to what your most serious competition is and should be able to
compile a 'league table' which shows who your closest five or six
competitors are. If there are only one or two, then you have chosen
the right market sector in which to specialize! If there are none at

all, then you have defined a particularly narrow and under-targeted niche group. However, this may also mean that your goods or service are not one that any other business has felt it would be worthwhile to sell. If it is an innovatory product and you are therefore the first in the field, all well and good. You will need to think carefully, however, if this is not the case. If it is goods or a service that are generally available offline, in normal retail outlets, why is no one else selling it on the web? If you have come up with a brilliant and original idea, and protected it with a patent or copyright, this means that you are much more likely to succeed in your venture but doesn't mean that there are absolutely no substitutes. There is always, in economic terms, the alternative of going without. If this is the only competition that you face, however, you could have a very successful product.

Perfect substitutes

In the case of perfect substitutes, you need to decide first whether you have the muscle to be able to enter an existing market. It may be that the market niche that you have chosen is already occupied. This does not mean that it is impossible for your e-commerce arm to start trading but does, of course, mean that success is going to be that much harder to come by. If you wanted to go into selling tulip and narcissi bulbs over the web and found that there was already a well-established purveyor of these items, then entering that particular market will be an uphill struggle. Perhaps you have no choice – if you are a business that deals in, for example, supplying garden products, then you can hardly start an e-commerce arm that deals in something completely different like roofing tiles. But you can think carefully about the range of products that you offer and concentrate on that range where there is least competition. If there is a competitor with a strong line in garden gnomes, then don't offer them over your web site, but concentrate on something else, like classical statuary. If you think that you have got the muscle to enter a particular market and find it already occupied, then check out the supplier. Can you get a better deal than the competitors so that you have a cost advantage? Can you use the leverage of your offline business to help you with your online one? If you have an excellent source of supply for your business, and one which relies heavily on your business, then you may be able to come to an arrangement so that you have greater cost effectiveness than a competitor's business.

In the case of close substitutes you need to look at the differences and similarities and, from a consumer's point of view, say which you think are positive and which negative. Your own product then needs to accentuate the positive and reduce the impact of the negative points. Again, you can categorize the competition by listing its good points and its bad points. Look also at the relative price ranges – are there cheap substitutes for your products or expensive ones? What is likely to attract a customer to an alternative? What are consumers looking for in this particular market – do they expect the product to be cheap or expensive, widely available or exclusive, weatherproof or not, in a particular colour, size or shape? All of these sorts of questions (and many others specific to the products that you intend to supply) can help to categorize both your goods and services and those of competitors.

Promotions and specials

In those markets where there is an identical product to yours, you need to have a strategy as to how you are going to distinguish yours from the competition. This is where the concept of added value comes in. If you can offer a little something extra for your customers – something over and above what the competition is willing to offer – then you can begin to carve out a market. This will no doubt mean incurring costs, in terms of time if not in terms of other things such as discounts, promotions and special offers. If this means that your e-commerce profits are likely to be curtailed, or that you may even start by making a loss on your e-commerce operations then you might be worried. However, the tactic of using the profits from your existing business is a well tried and tested one. Many Internet businesses have started with a huge cash 'burn' because of the amount of advertising or promotion that has been linked to the launch of their operation. Successful ones will gradually cut the burn rate down but will see it as an essential to building up a core to the business. It is a tactic that has a history of success in those businesses that could afford it – Sky Television made huge losses for many of the early years of its operations, but built up a customer base by giving satellite dishes and decoders away, amongst other expensive promotions. Once it moved into profit, it was able to consolidate its customer base, and quickly made up for all the loss-making years. During the loss-making period it had the benefit of being part of the News International group, who were able to finance the losses. If this is a tactic that you expect to use then you need to ensure that, in the same way that News International were able to cover the losses made by Sky, your losses are able to be covered from the profits of your existing business.

'But I particularly wanted New Zealand lamb for lunch on Sunday...'

Other markets

Because you are now selling online, you also have to look at the other markets that you have entered – not just the local, but also the national and international ones. It is important that you make it absolutely clear to visitors which markets you are willing to supply to. If you want the benefits of a worldwide market – with the large number of potential customers that is possible from even a narrow market niche – then you should be prepared to supply to as many parts of the world as possible. This is not as difficult as it may sound, with national post offices often providing a good and remarkably cheap service.

You may have the facility to take orders from The Philippines, Antarctica or the New Zealand bush, but do you have the ability to deliver? This will, of course, depend on exactly what it is that you are intending to deliver. Some goods or services are likely to be only wanted on a local or a national basis. An estate agency, for example, will get many more customers from its own 'patch' than from other parts of the world, and this business has the benefit that the product is unlikely to need to be moved! Local knowledge is also a pre-requisite for businesses supplying a service of this nature. Knowledge of language, customs and local property laws and conventions will be essential.

Some goods or services, as discussed in previous chapters, are unlikely to be suitable for delivery across the Internet, they may be too fragile, or too bulky, or just too expensive to transport. In the case of some businesses, common sense tells the consumer whether they are likely to deliver or not. I may be able to log on to the UK Asda (**www.asda.co.uk**) or Tesco (**www.Tesco.co.uk**) web site from Canterbury, New Zealand, or on to the Woolworth's site in New Zealand (**www.woolworths.co.nz**) from Canterbury in England, but I would be foolish to expect any of the businesses to deliver my groceries outside their own country. Other products may also present difficulties, in that they may require customs clearance or be subject to tariffs on entering another country. It is illegal to send some products by post and you must ensure that you are complying with both the laws of the country that you are operating in and the laws of the country where the goods are being delivered. So with a number of products it is probably not a good idea to suggest that you can ship it out worldwide for next-day delivery – not if it is dependent on local health or import regulations. However, even if you have made it clear that you are only selling in, say, a national market, you still need to check out the international competition. Just because you are being good enough not to sell your stuff in their back yard doesn't mean that they are going to be good enough not to compete with you on your own patch.

Visiting competitors

You can use normal business directories to start to see what sort of competition you might have online. Businesses will be listed with a web site address if they have one. Everyone will have e-mail but only some will list a site. You could start by looking at these sites and seeing what sort of level of service and range of products they supply. Check out prices, variety and delivery dates and see whether or not you can match or better them. Also check out how long it takes the site to load and whether there are any particularly striking or annoying features about it. Does it have a good colour scheme, for example? Is it successful in promoting a brand image? On the other hand, does it carry too much advertising or ask too much information from its prospective customers.

You will already know about local business directories and should have your own entry in one or more of them; these will be both general business directories and those which are specific to your type of business. (Don't forget to update your own entries with your web site address as soon as is practicable after it has launched on the web.) Search engines, similarly, act as directories, and there may be one that is specific to your line of business. This may be a more important source of information than general search engines.

Search engines

Online you can use general search engines by entering key words or phrases to do with your industry or product. You will need to understand how to narrow your search using the advanced search options if necessary. (For example, by using inverted commas around a phrase, you can ensure that only that exact combination of words or characters is thrown up by the search.) You should also use the services of specialist search engines which may produce a greater range of results. These are called metasearch engines which search other search engines and then produce a list of 'hits'. Metasearch engines allow a user to query several search engines at the same time. The better ones are able to cut out redundant responses. Some will have the ability to carry out searches in other languages and most provide a good help section to assist you in making your search as effective as possible. Some will be able to categorize your results, and all will list them by a percentage total that gives some idea of how relevant the site will be to your search (as do normal search engines). Metasearch engines include All4One, AskJeeves, DogPile, Infind, Metacrawler, Metagopher, Starting Point and Web Taxi (there are many others; you can search for them by putting 'metasearch engines' into your browser as an initial search). They will also tell you the sort of information which other searchers, asking similar questions, found useful. If you do a search on your product name or type you will see what web sites appear with which you are in competition. Start with the default search engine in your browser and then use each of the other search engines to which you have access. It is better to use several search engines as some businesses will appear near the top of one but not necessarily near the top of another. The major search engines for the global net are (in alphabetical order):

www.altavista.com	www.lycos.com
www.excite.com	www.northernlight
www.google.com	www.webcrawler.com
www.hotbot.lycos.com	www.yahoo.com
www.infoseek.go.com	

The main UK-based search engines include (in alphabetical order):

www.freepages.co.uk	www.ukplus.co.uk
www.searchuk.co.uk	www.yahoo.co.uk
www.ukdirectory.co.uk	www.yell.co.uk
www.ukindex.co.uk	

For the purposes of this exercise it is probably better to use the search engines themselves, in turn, rather than the metasearch engines – you can also decide whether you wish to search only in your own country (as with the UK-based search engines above) or would like a more global search. This will depend on the type of goods or services that you intend to offer for sale and on the markets that you are targeting. You will only really need to concern yourself with the top ten or so competitors which each search engine throws up, you can save or print the first page of 'hits' and then move on to the next search engine. Although it may seem like a bind at the time, it is probably better to print the information off as this will make it easier to handle and to cross-reference your lists. Do the exercise twice, to see if the same 'hits' appear the second time around (this won't always be the case) and also search using different terms and different products. Again, this will throw up different lists and in different orders. The best organized of your competitors (and therefore the one with which you are most likely to go 'head to head') will be the one that appears both the most times and the nearest to the top of the lists. Unfortunately the search engines will not tell you the most useful information, which is who those other searchers were!

It is also worth carrying out these searches on all the different search engines as they use different methods to categorize businesses. What may not turn up at all on one search engine may turn up at the top of the list on another. It may also be that there are search engines that carry particular categories, which will match with your market. If you have a list of your competitors (perhaps compiled from offline business directory type sources) and search for their presence on the Internet you will find what search engines they use and how easy it is to find their web sites. You can use **www.linkpopularity.com** to find out how many sites have already established links to those of your competitors – this will give you some indication both of how long they have been e-commerce enabled, and how popular the particular site is.

Benchmarks

The ease with which you can find these sites is your benchmark: you must be at least as easy to find as they are. Benchmarking means checking the performance of a plant, department or process against that of a competitor. The process of benchmarking involves identifying the best competitor – a suitable competitor offering similar products or product ranges to similar markets to yours – and then measuring performance in a number of key areas. In this case you need to use the comparison of competitor web sites that you have made, choose the best overall competitor, and make sure that your own web site operation matches it for quality, speed and reliability. You should try to improve on those areas where your competitor is doing better. Also, this is not a one-off exercise, but should be repeated at regular intervals so that you are always building on improvements.

It is possible to make the benchmarking exercise into a formal partnership with a business that is at a similar size and similar stage of development to yours, but not in direct competition. In this way you can share best practice. The Confederation of British Industry (**www.cbi.org.uk**) has set up a database called PROBE that helps companies to find suitable benchmarking partners.

Obviously you will need to spend some time looking at your competitors' sites and asking yourself a number of key questions. What would attract you to them as a customer? What would put you off? What do you think has been done particularly well or particularly badly? Then make sure that you don't make the same mistakes. It is also a good idea to become an online purchaser, just to see how well the system works and whether there are any bugs or problems that you should look out for. You could try purchasing from a competitor so that you can see what services are offered and how the sale is followed up. Make a list of the various stages of the transaction and then rate them for efficiency. This will give you a good feel as to how efficient the process is as a whole and also allow you to see which parts of the process might be either improved or done away with altogether. You can become an online customer with non-competitors – why not buy your office equipment online? Or even that new computer that you are going to need to run your e-commerce operation? What can go wrong? What does go wrong? And how would you make sure that any transactions on your site were smooth and problem free? You should also note how the site tries to add value. Is there, for example, a free newsletter service? Are you recognized as a customer if you visit the site again?

Intellectual property

Remember, however, that there are laws on intellectual property (see page 196). You should not copy anything directly from someone else's site – and this includes the layout or the method of presentation – nor can you 'lift' pictures or other details even though it may be really easy to do so. You may think that, because the site you are 'lifting' from is in Australia that its owners will never find out. But they will be doing exactly the same as you – checking out the competition – and will, inevitably, discover you. Moreover, it is dishonest and an immoral business practice. Only ideas are not copyright – layout, text, photographs, banners, templates, special colour schemes, logos, brand names, catch phrases etc. are all protected.

Other avenues

You could also employ an agency to find out what competitors are getting up to, but this is likely to prove expensive and, certainly in the case of the online research into competition, it is pretty straightforward (if somewhat time-consuming) to do it yourself. Other avenues include subscribing to online magazines (e-zines) and to your competitors' own mailing lists. If they do produce an e-mail newsletter, then you want to see it. You can then see what special offers or promotions are being offered and either try to spike them with alternative ones of your own or, more constructively, promote other products of your own that are not in direct competition with those being promoted. You could also monitor the number of times that competitors are mentioned in relevant newsgroups (see page 135). **www.tile.net/news/** will do a search of the newsgroup communities for you so that you can find out which company names, brands or product types have been a subject of discussion.

Customer feedback

One resource which you have for free is the feedback that you can get from your own customers. Use online feedback to see which of your competitors they have visited and how often. You can ask questions like, 'Have you bought this product from any other online supplier?' You can also ask customers to name the supplier – this will help to define your main competitors. Find out what has brought them to your site (a link, an advertisement, a search engine) and where else they shop. This also helps you to define and focus your niche as tightly as possible. Remember, it should be as narrow a market segment as possible – the narrower it is, the less likely you will face any serious competition.

Keep it ongoing

All of this research should be an ongoing process, updated as often as you can so that you are always aware of what competitors are doing and how you can best compete with them. Visit their web sites on a regular basis and see how they have changed or updated them (you will get a good measure of their efficiency and commitment to e-commerce by seeing whether they have changed or updated the site or not). Keep a close eye on any discussion forums which they have on their site. These are special areas of the site where visitors can ask questions, leave comments and hold discussions. These areas can be 'moderated' or not. If they are moderated then this means that messages are monitored by the site before they are posted. This stops the forum from becoming clogged up with useless, irrelevant or offensive comments. For an example, visit **www.schoolsnet.co.uk**, where you will find a number of discussions of an educational nature taking place, categorized by different subgroups. It should be part of your marketing strategy to have such a forum, relating to your own products and areas of expertise, on your own web site.

> **!** | **Hints and tips!**
> Collecting information on your competitors is a good way to find your way around the various search engines and see which of them most efficiently fulfils your needs. Normally, users stick with just one or two 'favourite' search engines, which this exercise will help to identify.

Web links

The main search engines are listed on page 104, and also in the section specific to search engines (page 181) so are not repeated here.

Three national based stores building e-commerce expansion into their existing businesses can be found at: **www.asda.co.uk**; **www.tesco.co.uk**; **www.woolworths.co.nz**

A useful site is **www.linkpopularity.com**, which shows the sites that have the most links – and where to.

The Confederation for British Industry, the organization for employers in the UK, can be found at **www.cbi.org.uk**

Also useful, **www.tile.net/news/** is the online reference to Usenet newsgroups, and **www.schoolsnet.co.uk** is a UK-based educational site.

Glossary

Business

burn rate   the rate at which a business burns (or spends) its initial capital; a high burn rate means that the cash is soon spent

substitute   a product that is in competition

perfect substitute   a product so near to yours as to be identical; try to avoid competing in this area

complement   products which are bought at the same time or to be used with your product

brand image   the 'message' which a business manages to give through logos, colour schemes, slogans etc.; linked to the values and aims of the business

intellectual property   the right of a person to assert that 'this is mine' and should not be copied

Information Technology

search engine   a free service provided on the web through which you can look for sites using key words or phrases

metasearch engine   a search engine that searches other search engines
discussion forum   an area on a web site where visitors can post questions or comments and expect replies
e-zines   online magazines

Summary

- Some industries are already conducting a large proportion of their business on the Internet. If this is your area of expertise, then you will face fierce competition.
- You should take account not just of competitors (selling substitute products) but also track how well complementary products are doing – their success will impinge on your success.
- Knowledge of competitors' products should extend to how close a substitute they are for your own products. The closer the substitute, the greater the competition. You should try to avoid competing with rivals who offer very close substitutes, at least until you are well established.
- Define your niche market as tightly as possible so that you are competing with as few other businesses as possible.
- See what added value your competitors offer and try to match or better it.
- Don't just check out national competition; look at all the markets that you have entered – you may not be selling in their markets, but they may be selling in yours.
- Visit competitors' web sites and judge them – find them by using search engines or online directories. Use all the major search engines so that you have as full a picture as possible of the opposition.
- Buy from competitors to see how smoothly the transaction is carried out.
- Learn from the good points and avoid the bad points in competitors' e-commerce operations, but don't steal anything from the site except ideas.
- Many techniques which you already use to find out about business competitors can be adapted for use online, including the use of agencies and of customer feedback.
- Checking out the competition needs to be an ongoing process.

8 | MARKETING STRATEGY

'I don't understand how a brilliant display like this is failing to attract customers!'

This chapter concentrates on marketing theory and on how this can best be applied to your marketing strategy. The practical aspects, in particular of marketing using the web itself, are covered in the following chapter.

Web invisibility

Many businesses have built and launched web sites and then wondered at the web phenomenon that is known as invisibility. It is easy to have a successful product in a chosen niche market but to find that a web presence is not attracting the sort of custom which you had hoped for. Indeed it may not be attracting any custom at all. This disappointing scenario can be as a result of any one of a number of different factors, not all of which are likely to be within your control. Some, however, will be, and it is these problems that you will need to address through your marketing strategy.

Most businesses immediately assume that they are not getting enough 'hits' because of the key words that they have chosen when registering on a search engine, because of the number of search engines on which they have registered, or because they have not chosen the 'right' or 'best' search engine. However, the invisibility may not be due to your position on search engines or the key words which you have chosen to use with them. It may be just due to the fact that your chosen market segment does not know that you are out there. This is not solely in terms of your business or company name but in terms of the product or range of products that you are selling. Customers are not finding you because they don't know to look for your product. They have yet to discover the wonderful benefits (or even existence) of whatever it is that is being targeted at them. How can this be so? And how can it be rectified?

Let's take an established product like the Sony Walkman as an example. This was what is called in business terms a 'product-led innovation' in other words the product was developed first (after intensive market research, of course) and the 'gap' in the market then created) through advertising and aggressive promotion, to contain the product. This is as opposed to a market-led innovation where a product is developed in order to fill an existing gap in the market. Waterproof material for clothing was developed as a response to people wanting to stay dry, rather than being invented and then marketed to people.

Publicity works

Without the appropriate publicity – which Sony, of course, had already prepared and budgeted for – nobody would have known of the existence of the Sony Walkman and therefore could not have gone into a shop and asked for it. The Sony distribution network, however, meant that, after localized test marketing, the product appeared in many hundreds of shops all around the world at the same time. Even without the advertising and promotion, the nature of the Walkman as a physical product being sold in real shops meant that people would see it and could try it and, if they liked it, not only buy it for themselves but recommend it to a friend. The success of the strategy is self-evident in the high sales and widespread use of the product. Many copies have also been spawned and variations on the original Walkman (such as the CD-playing Discman) have kept the product alive and growing. Does your product perhaps fall into this category? Is it so new or revolutionary that people are not looking for it because they don't yet know that it exists? Do they not demand your product because they aren't yet aware of its benefits? The Walkman is a classic example of a product-led introduction. Its benefits were clear to all who came across it. Does this apply to your product? If it does, then something has gone wrong with your marketing and you will need to return to the basic structure of the classic marketing mix and devise a new and effective marketing plan.

This is only one possible reason for the invisibility of your product. There are certain others that may also produce this phenomenon. Getting the link between target market and product right is an essential. For success you need to target the right product at the right market, and failure may therefore be to do with getting one half or other of this formula wrong. You may have the wrong product for your target market or, more commonly, have the right product but be promoting it in the wrong market. This is very easy to do when worldwide markets are on offer. You may not be aware of local customs or even news that can affect your market. What if you are, for example, trying to sell water filters in an area that prides itself on the purity of its water supply? Sounds unlikely? This is an actual case (the area actually bottled and sold its own spring water!). This is where good market research can make so much of a difference. You may be using the wrong strategy to sell your product – marketing it as cheap, for instance, when people expect it to be expensive: marketing it as being widely available when people want it to be exclusive. You could be trying to break into someone else's successful market and not be aware of the competition – another case of poor market research. Try selling a competitor to the Walkman for example and, apart from infringing intellectual property rights and finding yourself in a law court with

Sony lawyers, you will find it difficult to compete because the existing product is so well established. People will not bother to search for an alternative as they are quite happy with the product which they have already.

'Would the new one be better than the better one?'

How much marketing?

The amount of marketing that you have to do will depend on the nature of your product and the market that you are operating in. If it is a new product in a 'blue sky' market – i.e. one where there is no competition (like the Sony Walkman) – then marketing can be fairly minimal. If it is a new product in a competitive market, and a product that is at the beginning of its product life cycle, then it will require heavy marketing expenditure. If it is already a leading brand then it will require 'top up' advertising from time to time. In this last case it will be really important to transfer the brand image via the web site (see Chapter 11).

Product life cycle

Perhaps the product you are selling is in decline in terms of its product life cycle. It could have passed the point where it was popular and in high demand and even now be being replaced by a newer, cheaper or better alternative. A product normally goes through a period of initial growth which then flattens out as other competitor products begin to bite into the same target market. There follows a period of product maturity where sales remain steady, followed by saturation when competitor products flood the market or it may just be the case that 'everyone has got one' – imagine how many households in the UK are without at least one television, for example.

Figure 6

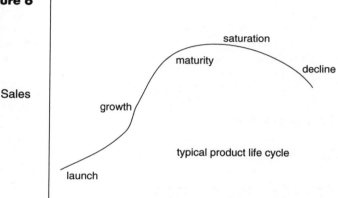

Figure 7

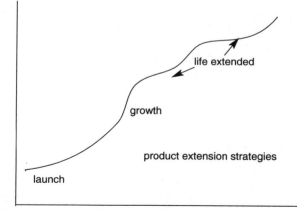

At this point the only way to maintain or increase sales is to change the product – introduce new varieties, develop different functions, change the product to a 'new' or 'improved' version. These are called product extension strategies. Televisions have become wide screen, surround sound, flat screen and so on. Or maybe the product has just 'had its day'. This is true of products other than those obvious ones taken over by technological innovation (gas lighting, for example). Consider the Japanese 'Tamagotchi' type toys which appeared in the mid- to late-1990s. These 'virtual pets' looked like they were going to eat into the toy market in a big way. They exploded on to the market and had a period of phenomenal initial growth, becoming a real 'craze'. But they faded and died, soon to be replaced by the next craze to come along (a common happening in the toy industry – be very wary if toys are your product line). Had you invested heavily in selling cyber pets (as they were called) over the Internet, you would have gained some initial success and then quickly found your market dwindling.

Finally, it is possible that the market you are entering is saturated, i.e. that there is no room for another competitor. If you are extending your real business on to the web, you will know with which products this is most likely to be the case, and these are the ones to avoid. Many of these problems can be, if not solved, at least forestalled by careful and professional market research (see Chapter 9).

But what if you've done your research – you have chosen the right market, you have an excellent product, you know that the people in your target market would buy your product ... if only they knew that you were there! Then you have a problem with your marketing and must look at how you can apply the traditional 'four Ps' of the marketing mix to your online sales. How can you raise the profile of your product?

The Four Ps

The classic 'four Ps' of the marketing mix are Price, Product, Promotion and Place, and the fifth 'P' – Packaging – is often added. You will need to look not only at these elements individually, but more importantly at the effect of a combination of them. If you are a pure Internet start-up then you need to begin by commissioning some good market research. You may feel that you can do this on your own or that a professional market research business will do it better. The professionals will be able to advise you as to what sorts of questions you should be asking and of whom, and will have the facilities for the interpretation of the data collected. But there is a great deal that you can do for yourself, much of it outlined in the chapter on competition (Chapter 7). Your computer and its Internet connection is, itself, a gateway to a huge store of published research, much of it carried out by large bodies such as local and national government agencies. Try **www.statistics.open.gov.uk** for UK statistics. This makes such research extremely accurate, and it is usually free. Even though it may not provide exactly the information that you require, it can give a wealth of valuable background data on your chosen market. You also have, provided as standard with most packages these days, the tools with which to interpret any other information that you collect. Microsoft Excel (and other spreadsheet packages) will produce graphs, charts and statistics to help you interpret data. (You may, of course, need help in interpreting the statistics!) Your main source of primary data (data that has not been published before, as opposed to secondary data, which has) should be the feedback which you receive from your own customers. This will not immediately be available to an Internet start-up business, but is a feature that can be built into your web site. Such information is available to businesses that are already trading but few seem to take advantage of it in any sort of scientific way. Whilst reacting to complaints (or praise) many businesses fail to systematically collect customer information and develop a policy for acting on it.

Some businesses (particularly in the service sector) have got the collection of and action on such information down to a fine art. Look at how a good hotel or airline, or an efficient car sales franchise, collects customer information and feedback, how they store it and how they act on it. Providing you are not in competition with them, they are likely to be happy to share their methodology with you. This collection of data from 'real' customers can easily be extended to your 'virtual' customers. Try to find out what sort of products they want, how frequently they will buy them, what their preferred price range is. They may tell you which of your competitors they use, how they found you, what attracted them to buy and whether they will come back again. All you need to do is build on the positives and try to eliminate the negatives!

If you are an existing successful business then part of that success will be as a result of listening to your customers and changing your marketing mix accordingly. You could try the same mix on the web-based part of your business but it is likely that, to be as effective as possible, you will need to alter it. On the web you should be targeting a particular niche market. A niche can actually be a great deal narrower on the web and yet still be bigger than anything that you have yet coped with. So, generally, the narrower the niche, the more focused is the target and the more effective your marketing. If you are a business start-up you will have to take care to start with a mix that is as near right as you can make it.

Market segmentation

Markets are divided into smaller and smaller parts or segments, with the smallest part being referred to as a niche. You will find that there are standard ways in which statisticians define markets (such as by socio-economic group). Most markets can be segmented by:

- **Geography** – tastes and wants will differ in different in different parts or regions of a country, or internationally. In China, for example, it is possible to promote the health-giving properties of certain parts of the tiger; in Europe this would be looked on with horror.
- **Demography** – the size, structure and trends in population. If you are targeting particular countries, the structure, in particular, can be an important factor. There may, for example, be many more divorcees and many single parents, creating a market niche. One growing group on the Internet is that of the so-called 'grey surfers'. These are retired people with both time and money who are happy with new technology and buying across the net.

- **Ethnography** – tastes and wants will differ amongst different racial and religious groups.

- **Behavioural considerations** – think about someone who might buy your product. Is it, for example, particularly new, fashionable, functional, glamorous, colourful, cheap or expensive? Will they buy it again (repeat purchases)? If so, how often and why?

- **Socio-economic** – this is usually categorized by household and based on the occupation of the head of the household. The groups in the UK are:

Class	Group	Typically
1	A	professionals, e.g. doctors, judges
2	B	managers, technical and executive, e.g. directors, accountants
3	C1	supervisory and clerical (non manual), e.g. secretaries, salespeople
3	C2	skilled manual e.g. electrician, plumber
4	D	semi-skilled manual, e.g. packers, assembly line workers
5	E	unskilled manual and low income groups, e.g. labourers, pensioners, students

In the UK, groups C1, C2 and D comprise almost three-quarters of the population and so are the most heavily targeted sector. Some of these characteristics can be linked – geo-demography, for example, links population characteristics with geographic areas.

Product

This is perhaps the single most important part of the traditional marketing mix, as outlined on page 116. The wrong product (or the right product aimed at the wrong market) will kill your Internet business before it has started. As we have seen, some products are just not suitable for selling across the web. This doesn't mean that you can't use your web site to try to get customers to come to your physical store, but this is hardly possible on a worldwide basis. Some services can be sold, particularly those that involve publication or telecommunication. For example, a document could be edited, a presentation written or a curriculum vitae composed. Services which have traditionally been available over the telephone – such as tipping services for betting on horse racing – can also be provided over the web. Over the telephone, a premium rate line might be the factor that makes the money; on the web it is more likely to be a subscription charge. **Lastminute.com**, a leading UK-based travel and entertainment site, changed its tactics by cutting advertising and concentrating on raising revenue through subscriber e-mails.

Services such as plumbing or electrical work can be advertised, but not sold directly (you can't mend a leak or replace a fuse over the web). You could also provide the service of hosting advertisements – this could be in addition to selling your own products. This only works, however, if you have a busy site that can guarantee traffic so that your advertisers know that they are getting value for money (the cost of a newspaper or television advertisement is closely linked to the number of people who will see it). Too many advertisements will just cause annoyance and may have the effect of visitors ignoring your site and going straight to other sites.

Products that sell

You can get a good idea of the sort of goods that will sell by looking at a successful catalogue retailer. However, you will need to remember that customers buy such goods in the knowledge that they can return those which are unwanted for any reason – no questions asked – and that the distribution system for both delivery and return is a tried and tested one. Are you willing to provide such a return guarantee on the products that you offer for sale?

Your products need to be exactly right for your target market, at the growth part of their product life cycle and easy to deliver to your customers. These are products that can be described and shown on the net, but only in two dimensions. The products which you offer need to have characteristics explained that would not need explaining if the customer could, for example, feel them, smell them, try them on, or do whatever is necessary to convince themselves of the quality of the product that they are buying. Products must be relatively easy to obtain from suppliers and your supply needs to be guaranteed.

Place

This really means distribution and distribution networks. To a retailer, place means not just the position and reputation of the outlets where products are retailed, but also the means by which the products can be distributed to those outlets. Traditionally, the trader sets up some sort of shop and the customer comes to him or her. This means that the trader needs to think about location, delivery, public services such as transport, the location of competition, and so on. Your Internet business does not face any of these traditional distribution problems, what it does face is the need to deliver the product to the customer, with the added difficulty that the customer could be located almost anywhere in the world. The catalogue retailer (as mentioned above) has the advantage of an established and reliable distribution system and a market that can be limited and defined by the areas where the catalogue is distributed (within a particular country, for instance). Your distribution system needs to be as strong as you can make it. Certain e-commerce businesses that have failed to make it have collapsed almost entirely due to their failure to deliver. There is nothing puts a customer off more quickly than shabby service or a failure to fulfil promises. Customers don't usually mind waiting for a product as long as it is not an excessively long wait. What they do mind is being told that it will arrive in two days and for it then not to turn up. Try to work out how quickly you can get a product to a customer. If it is worldwide delivery, you will have to talk to your national postal service, who should be able to offer a business deal of 'guaranteed delivery to any part of the world' for a certain price – then add on a couple of days to make sure that delivery is never late. If three-day delivery is guaranteed, then tell the customer 'delivery in five days' rather than 'delivery in three days' only to let them down on occasion.

Price

There are two possible economic models for pricing products on the Internet. On the one hand, the conditions found on the web could equate closely to perfectly competitive markets. The conditions of perfect competition are a homogenous product, free entry and exit into the market, many buyers and sellers, no single firm being able to influence price and that consumers have perfect information. On the web, consumers have perfect information – they can easily and quickly check prices on other sites – there is freedom of entry into and exit from the market and there are many buyers and sellers. There is no restriction on the number of businesses selling any particular product and it is difficult for existing players to raise barriers to market entry. Brands, patents and product differentiation are all still possible (for example, you could not sell Coca-Cola or Pepsi Cola on your site, but you could sell your own brand of cola), but only if sufficient profits are being made to pay for such branding and differentiation. The economics of perfectly competitive pricing should, according to some commentators, eventually mean that there will be no price competition on the web. Prices will be set at a level where a normal profit is made, consumers will choose the lowest-priced products and competitors will have to lower prices to this level in order to attract custom.

The other model says that each business on the web can actually use monopoly pricing. They can provide a product that is so differentiated or specialist – targeting a very narrow niche market – that there are, effectively, no competitors. In this case, the extra profits which are made can be used to support advertising, branding and further ways of making the product 'unique'. It is also possible that, at least in the short term, many businesses will use the profits from their 'real' business (where perfect or near perfect market conditions do not apply) to subsidize their web business.

Practical pricing

From a practical viewpoint, there are a number of ways in which you can price your products. Start by looking at your costs – is it cheaper to sell the product across the web than through traditional means? If so, then this should be reflected in your price. Look also at competitors' prices to see if you can match or better them. Techniques also include using loss leaders to gain initial market penetration. Can you afford to make a loss on web sales, subsidized by your existing business, until you have developed a reasonable customer base? Customers may be attracted by lower prices but will also react to the amount of value which you can add to their buying experience. You need to plan how you intend to add value (see Chapter 2).

Promotion

How do you make your site visible? It is worth thinking about the various ways by which you might promote a product sold in a real business. You could advertise it, using traditional media such as print (newspapers, magazines, trade journals, leaflets, posters and billboards) and direct mail. You could use broadcast media such as cinema, radio and television. Your decision as to which media to use would depend on its cost, on how easily and accurately it can be targeted and on how effective you think that it is going to be. So a small retailer might find that the local newspaper or radio station is the best way to gain visibility; a national concern might go for a television campaign or billboard advertising; a seller of products specific to a particular industry would concentrate on a trade journal. Other methods include direct mail (posting leaflets and offers to target customers) and 'cold calling' (telephoning people in the hope that they are in your target market – this is not very effective, and customers don't like it, the story of the lady who took great delight in inviting tradesmen round to measure up for a conservatory on her eighth floor flat is well worth remembering). All of these avenues are, of course, still open and can be used to help get people to your site.

Other sources

In the UK, use the *Yellow Pages* directory of businesses (**www.yell.co.uk**) or Thompson's local telephone directory (**www.thomweb.co.uk**) both to publicize your business and to find other routes through which you can publicize it. Look in trade journals, in newspapers and on the web for events. It is not just Internet related stuff that you are looking for but anything that can help you publicize your name and new web-enabled status. This may mean trade shows or exhibitions which have little or nothing to do with the Internet, but do have something to do with your business. How good are you at speaking in public? You must be reasonably good to be able to make a sales pitch so public speaking should come fairly easily. If you can speak in public then this is one way of spreading the word about your business locally. Often Chambers of Commerce and Chambers of Trade are seeking speakers. Give a talk on how to become Internet enabled, or how your business became Internet enabled (take this book with you if you like) and at the same time (of course) promote your own business and its web site.

Curiosity

One of the best weapons for many a site is curiosity. If you can promote your site address and a 'one liner' that describes your product in your target market then this will be worth doing. Television advertisements are effective and can actually be targeted on a fairly small area. You will be surprised as to how little a local television advertisement can cost. And cost is, of course, a major consideration. National advertising of any sort, be it newspaper, magazine, billboard, radio or television, is extremely expensive. Nor does the expense ensure success. You still need to make sure that it is reaching your own target market. Advertising that does not reach your target market is money that is clearly wasted. Define your market carefully, perhaps by industry, by geographic area (if you are targeting a particular part of the world), by interests, age, gender or income group. This is a vital part of your promotional technique. Then try to devise advertising and promotion that only reaches that market. You should define a primary market sector – your main target – and a secondary sector where you might pick up sales. This is not always as easy as it sounds. Does a seller of children's toys for example target the children (who don't have spending power but do have what is now termed 'pester power'), or does it target the parents (who do have spending power but are uninterested in the toys)? Look at your target market – where is the most powerful influence for buying your product? That is what you must target. Your secondary market may be people who would buy on occasion, or in some cases would buy to give to the primary market (men buy fragrances to give to women) or people who are just trying your product out. In the latter case it is the value which you add that will decide whether they become a part of your primary market.

You need to budget for all expenses. A proper and comprehensive marketing plan, with costings, is the only way that you should go about marketing your site. Many rely on a scatter-gun approach of 'we'll try this and see if it works' only to be met with expensive failure. Some pure dot.com start-ups have failed because they have spent far too much on promoting their site (and succeeding in getting their name extremely well known) and nowhere near enough on actual delivery. Remember, it is the marketing mix that is important; create an imbalance by concentrating too much on just the one element of it and you can soon find yourself in trouble.

Public relations is another aspect of promotion. This involves getting your name known through linking it with events or public figures. You should be part of events in your industry and can also hold your own events. The key to good public relations is to create an event that is news. Virgin owner Richard Branson's attempts to circumnavigate the globe by balloon obviously had something to do with his sense of adventure. Industry watchers might also have noticed that the Virgin logo and other information was always prominent, not just on the balloon itself, but on all sorts of other associated gear. You don't need a balloon, but could stage another event. How about a grand opening for your site. Or perhaps a competition for a valuable prize that requires contestants (prospective customers) to log on to your site? Of course, if you happen to know a celebrity who is willing to endorse your site…!

Packaging is often referred to as 'the fifth P' of the marketing mix. This refers to the way, for a web business, that you present your site. With a web site it is inevitably linked to the look of your site but also refers to the way in which products and their properties are presented. The words you use to describe your products need to be very carefully chosen – a fragrance seller might describe a scent as 'heady', 'fresh' or 'subtle'. In the physical world the consumer can test this; in the virtual world, the only evidence available is the label on the bottle. Descriptions – accurate ones – are therefore very important.

Price, product, promotion, place need to be applied as a mix – the marketing mix – to your web-based operations. You will already have a successful mix for your real business. However, it is not always possible (or desirable) to transfer this mix directly. What works well in your physical business may not always work so well in the web-based part. A whole new marketing strategy will be required. This means a proper, thought out and costed marketing plan.

? Did you know?

Competitions and guarantees are often used as devices to both increase sales and to gather information about customers. Offering a competition prize to customers who fill in a survey form may be more effective (and cheaper) than paying for market research. Customers can also be asked to fill out information on guarantees.

! Hints and tips!

Look at competition entry forms and at product guarantees produced by large businesses. They will have paid a lot of money to make sure that they are asking the right questions. You can get very good, very cheap advice on what sort of questions might be relevant for you by looking at what they ask.

Web links

For an example of a site selling entertainment, travel and gifts go to **www.lastminute.com**

For UK statistics go to **www.statistics.open.gov.uk**

The *Yellow Pages*, the UK business telephone directory, can be found at **www.yell.co.uk**

and **www.thomweb.co.uk** provides a commercial telephone directory of businesses and services.

Glossary

Business

blue sky market   a market with no competition as yet

gap in the market   a discovered or created 'gap' where demand has not yet been tapped

market-led innovation   a gap in the market for which a product is created or developed to fill it

marketing mix   the mixture of price, promotion, product and distribution used to increase sales

media   the way in which messages are passed from your business to your prospective customers

pester power   advertising term coined to describe the power that children have to persuade parents to buy

product extension strategies   changing, developing or upgrading a product so that sales can be maintained

product-led innovation   the product is developed first, then the gap in the market is created

product life cycle   the natural cycle that a product goes through from its initial launch to its final demise

top up advertising   advertising designed to reinforce an already established name or image

Information Technology

web invisibility   the phenomenon of establishing a web site and then not receiving the expected number of visitors

Summary

- Invisibility is a common problem on the web. Good marketing can overcome it.
- It may be caused by the nature of the product that you are selling.
- It may be caused by not targeting the right market segment effectively.
- It may be caused by choosing the wrong product or the wrong market segment.

- You can raise the profile of your product through careful marketing.
- This involves a marketing plan, which will suggest solutions to problems of price, product, promotion and distribution.
- You can use your existing business to subsidize your web operation but this needs to be done with care.

9 | USING MARKETING TECHNIQUES

'I think that's everything covered.'

Marketing the site

Rather than concentrating on the theory of marketing, this chapter looks at some of the practical aspects of it, in particular the use that you can make of the web itself to help with your marketing strategy.

The fact that you have arrived on the web will not be immediately obvious to your customers unless you market the site using all the online and offline techniques and avenues that are available to you. Firstly, let the existence and location of the web site be known by using the web address on everything printed that goes out of your business. (This is the URL, the Universal Resource Locator, now commonly referred to as the 'dub, dub, dub'.) You should also include it in your company livery and, if applicable, on the side of vehicles and other assets. And don't forget entries in business directories, in telephone directories and in other advertising material such as the outside of envelopes. (It is easy to set up software so that your company name and web site address is printed at the same time as you print customer addresses on envelopes). Add it also to your e-mail headers. In fact, include it wherever you possibly can!

To make your staff feel a part of the venture and to include them in the publicity, make sure that you have business cards printed up with the web site address on them. This is also good for staff morale – it's often the little things that help make people feel a part of the business that can be important. You will also need to order new stationery – put your web address on it and on all your correspondence; make it prominent and, where space allows, try to let the reader know what they might find there. Your web address, on its own, is not enough information. You should also include a few well-chosen words which describe your business or its vision. 'Visit whatever.com for information, advice and discounted sales of whatever' is far more effective than just, 'Visit whatever.com'. Think of the key words that might make you enter a shop: 'full range', 'discounted sales', 'speedy service', 'personal service' and see how many you can adapt and adopt for a catchy introduction to your web site. Many businesses commit the cardinal error of not letting the casual reader know what line of business they are in. If this is not included in the name (footballboots.com, for example, gives a pretty good idea of what the business is trading in) then it needs to be included in a rider or tag-line which always follows the web site address.

Advertising

You don't have to limit your advertising to the traditional channels. There are more ways of advertising your presence on the web that are available to you once you are online. Some are fairly obvious, and will need to be paid for; others are more subtle, possibly more effective, and yet free. Amongst the more obvious are paid-for advertisements on other web sites and the use of banner advertisements. Less obvious (and cheaper) include introducing yourself and your product to discussion groups and newsgroups and using your own customers for marketing purposes.

Paid-for advertisements

Visibility can be achieved through high levels of paid-for advertising (with the consequent high levels of expenditure) but this does not, of course, guarantee profitability. According to research published at the start of 2001 by PriceWaterhouse-Coopers, most B2C businesses will run out of money – i.e. run through their initial funding – in less than a year and a half, many well inside this time frame. At this point they then have to go 'cap in hand' to investors and entrepreneurial providers of risk capital in order to top up the funding. The plan (often more a hope than a plan) is that sales will eventually overtake the expenditure. This is not a course that is recommended for the typical small business which is expanding on to the web. You will need to be extremely careful about the levels of advertising expenditure that you can support, and have a clear idea of how much you are willing to spend in order to achieve a certain level of sales. Because, often, the hopes that went with the initial expenditure have been dashed, and the market is in the period of uncertainty (defined by the diagram on page 2), many start-up e-commerce enterprises have found it difficult to obtain risk capital. If you can finance the marketing for the expansion from your own existing business then this is, without doubt, the best course of action – providing that you do not stretch the resources of that business too far. You do not want your e-commerce operation to bring down your established business. (Don't forget that, if your e-commerce business is a straightforward extension of your existing business, the assets of the 'real' side, should there be problems, can be used to pay off the debts of the e-commerce side. Otherwise, if you are not incorporated as a limited liability company, your own personal wealth and assets are at risk.)

Web-based marketing

The lowest-cost advertising is likely to be actually on the web. The most obvious way in which to market your site on the web is through the use of banners. These are statements regarding the whereabouts of your site and what it does that are placed on other web sites. They can be very colourful, striking and animated and can also be hyper-linked directly to your site. Constructing a banner is not difficult. For clear instructions go to **http://webservices.adobe.com/banner/main.html**. Your banner can be saved to your own hard drive and then transferred to anywhere on the web. You could join a banner exchange association where your site hosts advertisement banners for a partner site and they host yours, although remember that being faced by a barrage of advertising can end up putting potential customers off. Often more established sites will also require a 'two for one' deal where they will host your banner for free, providing that you host two of theirs. This may be a good way of getting traffic to your web site but you should also be very careful about how you choose your partners. Be certain that they are not promoting or selling anything that might either compete with your business or be detrimental to its image.

Incentives

A statement to the effect that 'we are at www.whatever' should be included in each banner as a minimum, plus a brief phrase to give an idea of what you do. Sometimes this is obvious (e.g. Harry's Health Food Shop), sometimes less so (e.g. Harry's). Presenting this information is a start, but what you really want is some sort of incentive for people to visit. So, for example, you could say 'log on to www.whatever for more information on whatever' or 'click on www.whatever for discount vouchers' or 'visit us at www.whatever for your free information pack'. The second and third examples are more effective than the first one. The first one offers little incentive (it does at least offer some, so is better than just the bare statement that 'our web site is at www.whatever'). The second one offers a tangible reward for visiting the site in the form of discount vouchers, the third does even better by actually getting the customer to register with the site.

Attracting advertisers

A further way to raise your profile (and also a way of generating more revenue) is to attract other advertisers to your web site. Your site is, after all, a publication, and any advertisements on it will be read by your visitors. You can therefore charge to carry advertisements providing you can present evidence to advertisers of the type and number of visitors which your site may have.

To contact likely advertisers you will have to use, to a great extent, good old-fashioned offline techniques. If you were launching a magazine which concentrated on mountain biking then your first recourse for information on advertisers would be a selection of rival magazines. You would look at the businesses which advertised in them, who appeared to spend the most money, who appeared the most often across the selection, who appeared to take out the biggest, most colourful and most expensive advertisements. You would then obtain a list of advertising rates (either printed in the publication or obtainable separately from the publishers) along with the appropriate circulation information. There are published directories (such as BRAD, British Rate and Data, in the UK) to help you and a wealth of online information, as outlined below. Armed with this information, your magazine could then approach the advertising managers of each of the advertisers to offer a better deal than the one that they are already getting. You can follow the same process for your web site. Look at competitor web sites and see which is carrying advertising and from whom. You can then contact these advertisers to see if they would be willing to post an advertisement on your site.

Collecting information

The information that you are not likely to have in the online world is the number of visitors a rival site has, nor what they charge per advertisement. You can find this out by setting out to buy advertisement space on a rival's site. You just need to make enquiries as if you wished to purchase some advertising space – say that you have noticed that they carry advertising, and you would like to know the rates and their 'circulation'. This will give you a good idea of what you may be able to charge on your own site. Many sites carry 'hit counters' which show how busy the site is but, as commercial information, advertising details should be easily obtained by offering to place an advertisement on their site. You will also need to collect the information about your own visitors that advertisers will need to know. You can define your visitors by socio-economic group and other market segments by getting them to respond to an online survey. You can devise a simple survey form for visitors but will need to include some sort of incentive to get them to fill it in. For customers – those who actually buy a product – you should make sure that you collect the relevant information from them when they purchase from the site. You will also need a web counter, so that you can show the number of visitors to your site.

It is important that you are aware of the balance between content and advertisements. In a newspaper or magazine, it is easy to skip advertisements and find the content that you really want to read. This is not always the case on a web site. It may be that your advertisements actually take so long to load, or take up such a proportion of your site, that visitors quickly tire of visiting and withdraw to other sites.

Survival

Your advertising expenditure may be crucial in providing you with the 'visibility' that means that your web traffic will increase to a level where it is generating enough revenue to support the business. The balance between advertising expenditure and revenue generation is, however, not an easy one to achieve. It is worth bearing in mind the sort of figures which point to possible survival in the new markets. Many Internet start-up businesses have found themselves spending a great deal more on advertising than the income that they have achieved in sales. If it costs you more per unit sold on advertising than is generated in sales then you will be burning cash (i.e. using up your reserves and becoming reliant on fairly rapid growth of sales in order to make up the shortfall). If you have to spend, for example, £1.10 on advertising to gain £1 worth of sales revenue then you are probably spending too much.

(Probably, but not necessarily, as it depends on whether you can sustain the growth in your sales; some businesses spend as much as £1.25 on advertising for each £1 of revenue earned and still manage to survive – it's a question of balance and financial backing.) You will also need to have good gross profit margins on the lines which you offer over the Internet. Often, a business may be able to sell at a price which is four to five times the initial cost of the product. Margins which are less than this will leave you struggling. Typically, a failed Internet company will have been subsisting on margins of 65 per cent or below. It is also essential, as has been stated before in this book, that you have business acumen, experience and expertise. Those who come to the Internet with no business experience or training are much more likely to fail than those who know business and its risks. Part of that business acumen should ensure that you are competing in a well-defined and targeted niche market, but one where sales growth is still possible.

The best, cheapest and most effective method of promotion for many a site is, however, word of mouth. If associates within your field or industry see the site, see that it is good, and recommend it to others, then your traffic will not only increase but so will your trade as these are people who have specifically logged on to your site rather than gone through a search engine. (Getting your site registered with search engines and getting it to the top of the list is discussed in Chapter 12.)

Newsgroups

The Internet is not just the World Wide Web, as you already know, but also supports communications such as e-mail, chat rooms and newsgroups. Newsgroups can be a particularly useful way in which you can market your business online. Newsgroups provide subscribers with the opportunity to share special interests and to discuss specialized hobbies with other subscribers around the world. They may be based on a hobby, an interest or an industry – the ones that are the most useful to you will be those which have a direct connection with the business that you are in. Each group has its own site for posting news and views called a bulletin board and will be open to comments and conversation from new visitors.

So, whether you are a manufacturer of playing cards, bridge systems or bridge scoring devices, or involved in nursing and health care, or providing spares for motor cycles, there is a newsgroup – in fact a selection of newsgroups – that will be discussing problems and issues to which you may be able to provide product solutions. (In the case of these examples, for bridge-playing newsgroups visit **www.blakjak.demon.co.uk/br_ngrps.htm**, for nursing and healthcare newsgroups visit **www.shef.ac.uk/~nhcon/nunews.htm**, for motorcycle discussions visit **http://dir.groups.yahoo.com/group/HD-TC88**; please note that these are not chosen for any significant reasons, but are just random examples.)

How can you use your access to these newsgroups to promote your business? First you will need to find the newsgroup or selection of newsgroups which is or are most likely to be of use to you. You can do this by going to one of the newsgroup hosts, for example starlink newsgroups at **www.ast.cam.ac.uk/starnews/** or the homepage of the UK-based Usenet newsgroups at **www.usenet.org.uk/**. Usenet hosts an enormous number of newsgroups and you should not be surprised to discover that there are several, sometimes dozens, that relate to your product area or expertise. You could also try **www.tile.net/news/** which contains a comprehensive reference and archive to all usenet discussion groups, categorised by title and description. Other hosts include google at **http://google.groups.com** and yahoo at **http://groups.yahoo.com**. (Note that, when entering these addresses, some are not actually on the World Wide Web so do not need the 'www' prefix.)

However, the visitors to these newsgroups tend to be fairly jealous of their invulnerability to commercial entreaties and are likely to react badly to a direct sales approach. You will need to be patient and you will need to be subtle. Gaining the trust of a particular group can be a slow process but one which is worthwhile; losing trust within a particular newsgroup usually means that there is no chance of regaining it. Remember, conversations are already taking place and the group may have well-established members and well-established rules for how conversation is to be conducted. This is no different to real life. You should follow the same sort of rules as you would in entering a normal conversation. This means spending some time listening before offering to make any comment. This is even more important if, as is the case with a newsgroup, the conversation is between people who are strangers to you but not to each other. The advantage of 'listening in' to conversations in a newsgroup is that no one knows that you are there. It is not like hanging about on the edge of a crowd at a party trying to find an opening. Moreover, should the newsgroup not, in your opinion, turn out to be any use to your business, then you can quietly withdraw without anyone being any the wiser. There are always many other newsgroups that may be of use to you.

Promotions

You could also use newsgroups for promotional purposes by being prepared to give something away. Say you are a UK-based business that has invented a clip-on device that turns a normal light into a fog light for motor cycles. You could access a newsgroup for motorcycles at, for example,
http://dir.groups.yahoo.com/group/HarleyTC88 or
http://dir.groups.yahoo.com/group/HD-TC88, which you might have found by searching the database of newsgroups at **http://groups.yahoo.com**, and see if there has been any discussion on this matter. You will notice if you visit these groups that, although their discussions are on very similar matters, one of these groups is open to members only, the other has public access. Yahoo also shows the size of membership for each group. Alternatively, you could access the newsgroup to see if there is any discussion, find that motorcyclists are complaining about the lack of fog lights for bikes, and then produce one. You could offer a free trial of your device to the first ten people in the newsgroup who have complained about the problem and then, legitimately, report back the results of the trial. If the trial is a success, you will have yourself and ten other newsgroup members recommending your particular product. This is a strategy that can be copied into almost any newsgroup. Spot a particular problem that is causing people in the newsgroup concern and then offer a solution. Don't, as emphasized before, offer to sell the solution directly – you need to take a subtle and low-key approach within a newsgroup. Each message that you post has room for a signature line, or sig. line.

You can use this to announce who you are and what you do by making sure that the sig. line contains your URL and a brief statement of your business identity. For example, 'L'Avenir at **lavenironline.org** for quality educational training and consultancy' is more than enough to identify the business, explain what it does and let members know where on the web they can find it (L'Avenir is the author's business). The whole point of web-based business is that the customer comes to you rather than you going to the customer . It is what is called a 'pull strategy' rather than a 'push strategy' – but you must pull gently otherwise there will be resistance.

You could, of course, start your own newsgroup. Anyone can set up a newsgroup on a subject, even though that subject may be already covered by other newsgroups. Just because one group is having a conversation about something doesn't mean that another group can't start their own conversation. To start a newsgroup go to **http://groups.yahoo.com/** or **www.topica.com** where you can start a newsletter or discussion group for free.

Netiquette

There is a certain etiquette (netiquette in net terms) to conducting conversations and postings on the web. The use of capital letters is considered to be shouting (and therefore rude), for example. Other problems are the reliance that we have on facial and body language clues when conversing with other people. Humour may be misunderstood, because there is no opportunity for sounded laughter (the 'laughter track' pasted over television comedies is there to give us the clues that we might otherwise miss). And there is no opportunity to 'take back' what you have said if you send it hurriedly or without thought. The mistake, insult or gaffe will be there for all to see in black and white. There is a site at **www.albion.com/netiquette/corerules.html** which outlines the main rules for electronic communication.

Communities

There are also other online communities that you can approach with offers and promotions, in areas where you may also be able to advertise directly. These include major content providers. Many ISPs will provide their own content, available to members, and some have built huge 'communities' of members within their own content area. Some of the biggest are the communities created by Netscape, Compuserve and AOL (America online). These are members' communities and you will need to be a member in order to access them; however, there is usually a free trial offer for thirty days so that you have chance to familiarize yourself with the set-up before joining. (Don't forget that, as with many of these offers, you may need actually to cancel your membership rather than just stop visiting. The trial offers are usually set up so that you automatically take up membership if you don't positively cancel it by the due date.) These communities can be found at **www.netscape.com**, **www.webcenters.compuserve.com/ compuserve/menu/default.jsp** for non-members, and **www.aol.com**. (CompuServe is actually a subsidiary of AOL.)

Subscriptions

You can also both collect and disseminate information through subscribing to mailing lists and e-zines. When joining a community or newsgroup you will usually be given the option of subscribing to its mailing list. This means that you can be informed of any new discussions or items of interest on the site through your e-mail – rather than having to monitor the group closely yourself. (Should the amount of such mail that you receive become disproportionate to its usefulness, there will also be instructions on how to unsubscribe to such mailings.) E-zines are online magazines and, just like offline ones, will vary enormously in quality and usefulness. You can search by category or subject area so that, for example, a search on 'e-zines for marketing' will throw up a range of e-zines with marketing tips and advice such as the UK-based site **www.newbusiness.co.uk**, or the more international **www.newmediazero.com**. The first contains advice and information on online marketing, while the second concentrates on interactive marketing, advertising and publishing on the web. There are many, many more. Try **www.esearch.ie/ezineslist.jsp** for a comprehensive list of free e-zines or

www.smithfam.com/news/newsletter.html
for advice on how to use e-zines, or
www.webmarketingtoday.com/webmarket/ezines.htm for many
links to e-zines and other marketing resources.

Mailing lists

These are similar to newsgroups in that they involve postings of
information and comments that can lead to discussions. The
difference is that they don't take place in a 'forum' that you visit,
but are e-mailed directly to you. This means that subscribers
receive regular information of interest to them. In this way they
may be considered as acting like a newsletter. Most lists can be
subscribed to for free although some – usually containing
commercial information – will be charged for. A database of UK
and European lists is held at **www.list-link.com/default.asp**.
Direct mail news regarding these lists is available free only for a
two-week trial period, it then costs £59 per month. At
www.topica.com/ you will find categorized lists of newsletters,
which can also be found at the newsgroup hosts given above. Visit
these sites to create your own lists or newsletter.

Your e-mail newsletter can be forwarded to your subscribers and
contain details of new products, innovations and offers. You will
only be sending it to people who have subscribed – and therefore
declared an interest – so they are likely to be interested in your
products and quite happy to receive commercial details and
information. Limit your newsletter distribution to around ten to
fifteen times a year, otherwise your subscribers are likely to get fed
up with receiving it and unsubscribe. Obviously, you should always
have something new and fresh to say in it.

Information databases

Being on the net also gives you access to a great deal of
commercial information, compiled by professional organizations,
that could be of use to you in framing your marketing strategy.
Again, some of this will be free, some will be free for a trial period
and some will be for sale. Worldwide Forrester Research, based in

Massachusetts, USA, is a major player in terms of providing such information related to Internet businesses (go to **www.forrester.com**). In the UK this organization has joined forces with Fletcher Research and is to be found at **www.fletch.co.uk**. Forrester Research also links with the Hoover's web site at **www.hoovers.co.uk** which hosts links to over 14,000 companies, with information on their top personnel, competitors and finances coupled with a description of the business. UK-based information can also be found at **www.thebiz.co.uk** and with established providers of business statistics and information such as Dunn and Bradstreet at **www.dunandbrad.co.uk**.

There are also, of course, mailing lists and newsgroups specializing in statistical information. These can be found at **www.stats.gla.ac.uk/cti/links_stats/lists.html**.

Customer feedback

Your own customers and site visitors are also an important source of information. You could use a focus group or similar to give you feedback on the site. This does not have to be professionally constituted but could consist of friends and family, a group of fellow business people or a group of customers. In each case you must be sure to emphasize that you want honest feedback – whether negative or positive – and constructive criticism. In some cases you may have to make a small payment to keep people doing this job for you. This could comprise special offers or discount deals for chosen customers. You could make them special by giving them an identity – for example, call them 'gold customers' and allow them certain privileges, you'll be amazed at how much reward can be reaped from what is basically a tiny outlay. Detailed feedback can be obtained by using a customer response form to collect information about how people found their way to your site and what they thought of it when they got there. You can design an appropriate questionnaire form, target a group, send the form and interpret and analyse the information collected by using the tools at **http://zoomerang.com**. The service can be trialled for thirty days and fees then become payable.

! Hints and tips!

It is often a rule in business that if you 'give a little' you can get a lot back. This is a rule that can be applied to your web site. In return, for example, for a minor product of yours being delivered to them, you can gain a customers' details, possibly their loyalty and be able to contact them with new product offers and so forth. A little, in business, often goes a long way.

Web links

For bridge-playing newsgroups go to **www.blakjak.demon.co.uk/br_ngrps.htm**; for nursing and healthcare newsgroups visit **www.shef.ac.uk/~nhcon/nunews.htm**; for motorcycle discussions (on Harley Davidsons) visit **http://dir.groups.yahoo.com/group/HD-TC88**. Also mentioned in this chapter are **www.ast.cam.ac.uk/starnews/** – starlink newsgroups – and **www.usenet.org.uk/**, the homepage of the UK-based Usenet newsgroups.

A useful site is **www.tile.net/news/** which contains a comprehensive reference and archive to all usenet discussion groups.

Other newsgroup hosts include **http://google.groups.com**; **http://groups.yahoo.com**; **www.topica.com/**.

For the construction of a web site banner go to **http://webservices.adobe.com/banner/main.html**

For advice on netiquette go to **www.albion.com/netiquette/corerules.html**, which outlines the main rules for electronic communication.

The homepage for the Netscape content provider can be found at **www.netscape.com** and **www.webcenters.compuserve.com/compuserve/menu/default.jsp** is homepage for CompuServe non-members.

The America online homepage is at **www.aol.com**.

E-zines on marketing include **www.newbusiness.co.uk** and **www.newmediazero.com**. For a comprehensive list of e-zines use **www.esearch.ie/ezineslist.jsp**. For advice on how to use e-zines use **www.smithfam.com/news/newsletter.html**. Also, **www.webmarketingtoday.com/webmarket/ezines.htm** hosts many links to e-zines and other marketing resources.

Market and industry research organizations include **www.forrester.com**, **www.fletch.co.uk**, **www.hoovers.co.uk**, **www.thebiz.co.uk** and **www.dunandbrad.co.uk**.

Mailing lists and newsgroups specializing in statistical information are at **www.stats.gla.ac.uk/cti/links_stats/lists.html**.

Design a questionnaire form, target a group, send the form and interpret and analyse the information at **http://zoomerang.com**.

Did you know?

There are a great deal of jargon words used on the web, but the web can also provide the translations! There are 'jargon busters' at **www.whatis.com** and on the BBC site at **www. bbc.co.uk/webwise/glossary**.

Glossary

Business

tag-line   a catchy phrase that identifies your business

risk capital, venture capital   money which investors are willing to risk

BRAD   directory of publications with circulation figures and advertisement prices; expensive to buy and generally available in the reference section of your local library

margins   a measure of the amount of profit that can be made on a sale

pull strategy   getting the customer to come to you rather than you going to the customer

Information Technology

URL   Universal Resource Locator, your specific home on the web

dub, dub, dub   the shortened version for the 'www' prefix to web URLs

sig. line   your signature or identifier in newsgroups

netiquette   the accepted rules and conventions when conversing online

Summary

- There are a number of practical aspects to marketing your site using both offline techniques and online tools and information.
- Offline, it is important that your web site gets as much publicity as possible through the normal avenues of your own staff, stationery and literature.
- Online you can either pay for advertisements or look for other, less expensive ways to market your site.
- Banners can be used to advertise your web site; these can be exchanged with other sites.
- Incentives can be used to attract visitors to your site.
- You can host advertising if you have a large enough 'hit rate' (circulation).
- Advertising expenditure cannot be allowed to outstrip revenue for long if the business is going to survive.
- The most effective advertising is through 'word of mouth' and recommendation.
- You can introduce your business into newsgroups, but will need to take a 'softly, softly' approach.
- You can use newsgroup members to target promotions.
- Mailing lists, newsletters and e-zines can all be used either to collect or disseminate information.
- Professionally collected and collated market information is available on the web.
- Your own customers can help your marketing by giving you feedback.

10 | PRACTICAL STEPS IN SETTING UP

'... but how do I know that there isn't a piece missing?'

This chapter looks at the practical steps which a small business will
have to consider taking before building and launching an e-
commerce extension via a web site. It looks at the way in which
you decide to access the Internet and at establishing a brand
presence by buying a domain name. Firstly, you will need to think
about the way that you are going to access the Internet yourself.
Because you are accessing it commercially, this may be different to
what you would do if you were just accessing it as an individual. If
you have staff working for you, you will also need to think about
the way that your staff are going to access the Internet. This
includes deciding which of your staff are going to have access and
to what, and whether you are going to remain in overall control of
the e-commerce operation or delegate it to a member of staff. How
important is your time to the business? Can you afford to be your

own webmaster and build, develop and maintain your web site to run your e-commerce operation as well as your real-world one, or would it be better for you to use someone else? If you choose to delegate, the question then also arises as to whether it is to someone who you already employ, who has the expertise, or whether you will employ someone from outside your organization. You may be lucky enough to have someone on your staff who has the necessary skills – you will often find, as use and familiarity with the Internet grows, that you have someone with at least some knowledge of what is required. Even if you would like to write and launch a web site yourself, you may still need some expert advice about the sort of system which you need. Free advice from local or national government is usually available. In the UK, this is at **www.ukonlineforbusiness.gov.uk**; in the USA it is at **www.sba.gov**.

Connections

You will need different levels of connectivity depending on whether you are on your own or whether you have more than one machine in a small office. It may be that, in answering enquiries, collecting information or taking orders, you would like more than one member of staff to be able to access the Internet at any one time, and you would like them to be able to access it from their own machine. If you are on your own then you can connect directly via any one of the ways discussed in the opening chapters. Depending on the amount of use you will make of it, and the sort of speed and efficiency you require, you can start by having a straight dial-up connection via a modem, meaning that you have to dial your provider every time you want access. If this is your starting point then you must make sure that you have at least a 56K modem. If you are working on an older machine you may well find that it has one with a slower speed and will need to be upgraded. (On a machine running MS Windows look in the **Start** menu and choose **Settings**, **Control Panel**, **System** and **Modem** to see what is currently installed.) If you are going to need a faster and more efficient connection then you can install ISDN, ASDL, CDMA, cable or similar (depending on what your telecommunications provider can offer you), all of which will give you a permanent connection to the Internet – so no need to dial up for a connection – for a flat annual or monthly fee.

Local Area Networks

You will need different hardware if you have a small network (a local area network or LAN). In this case you will need to connect your LAN to the Internet using two essential pieces of kit, the hub and the router. A router will send and receive data for you. It is a clever little box that decides what the best and most efficient route (hence the name) is for data via the Internet and your own network. It is also the point on your system where you can have security devices built in, for example to prevent unauthorized access to your system. A hub, on the other hand, can be thought of as the points of a star or the spokes on a wheel. To each of the points you can connect a device – this might be a PC, a scanner, a printer or other device. The main drawback of this system is that only one device can send or receive data at any one time. Each point on the star (or spoke on the wheel) is sharing access via the central point – the hub – meaning that if one stream of data is passing, say, to one of your PCs, any other streams of data, say from a PC to a printer, or from a scanner to a PC, will have to wait. So where for a single machine you can have a direct link to the Internet via a modem, for a small group of networked machines you would have the router linked to the Internet, the hub to the router and the devices to the hub. You will still want the router to be linked via an ISDN or other digital device. ISDN, ASDL and cable are all digital (this is what makes them so much faster), whereas modems are only capable of handling analogue signals. Analogue signals can be interfered with by line noise, and can be interrupted and slow. Digital signals are clearer and also provide a much faster download time. For bigger businesses, who are either confident of their growth on the web or who have already grown, the switched LAN is the next option. This works like a hub in that it connects network devices to each other. However, unlike a hub, it allows a number of devices to send data at the same time. If you are going to use a hub or a switched LAN you will need to make sure that you have a digital connection; analogue connections will not be able to carry the traffic.

Peer-to-peer connections

Instead of a LAN, where machines are linked by a server, peer-to-peer communication allows one PC to talk to another without the intervention of a central hub or server. Some companies are adopting it as it can lead to increased usage time of their technology. If, when a worker goes home, his computer can still be remotely accessed by another worker (perhaps in a different time zone) then work can continue. It effectively means that everyone in the person to person 'wheel' is able to share the same database of information. This has obvious advantages for a business. One advantage for e-commerce is in supply – you can keep in constant touch with your suppliers and any other business partners without risking any information of a sensitive nature leaking into the public domain. The system can also be used for collecting online payments as it can facilitate person-to-person direct payments.

Electronic shop fronts

It may be, if you are just starting out on the web, that you need go no further than what are called electronic shop fronts. These are also known as e-malls. Many major hosts carry e-mall facilities. This is a little bit like taking possession of a lock-up shop in a shopping centre. Your business will be able to trade from a position alongside a number of other businesses for which you will pay a fee or a percentage on each transaction to the owner of the mall. The advantage of this system is that your transactions are taken care of and you do not need a lot of investment in order to be able to start selling your product online. The disadvantage is that you are just one of a number of shops in that particular e-mall – and some of the others may be competing with you as e-malls tend to concentrate on particular product types – and you will have difficulty standing out from the crowd. It is, however, a low-risk strategy that can be used to test the market for product sales before going to the time and expense of building and launching a full blown web site operation. Examples of operators can be found at **www.dkg.net** and **www.perquiro.net**.

Other considerations

At this stage you will need to consult the business plan you made earlier. In this you should have made decisions about how far down the 'electronic road' you want your business to actually go. Look at all the elements of your existing business and decide whether or not each element can be enhanced by making it electronic or by adding an e-business or e-commerce side to it. Can you make better use, for example, of e-mail or online marketing, will the use of EDI bring any advantage for your business? This will also help you to decide better what level of sophistication you will need for your e-commerce set up – do you need a full-blown web operation or can you take advantage of the new technology in other ways? You will also need to look at where your system might have a tendency to break down. Your system is only as strong as its weakest link – if you have a server with a tendency to crash or a PC that is short of memory, then this can seriously impair the whole operation. (This applies to the physical and logistical side of the business as well.) Governments are keen to see businesses using the potential of the Internet so you will also find that, in many cases, your government will provide a free service of help and advice (see page 146).

Choosing an access provider

An access provider is an organization that will connect you to the Internet. It will provide you with web space where you can place your web site and will also have its own e-mail services, news and content services, amongst other things. Usually you will be connected via an ISP. You may decide, however, that it is not an ISP (Internet Service Provider) that you need but an ASP (Application Service Provider).

ASPs

Application Service Providers are similar to ISPs except that they tend to concentrate on the business side of the net and supply applications that fit the needs of businesses. They can provide ready-made and tested applications to carry out common business functions such as accounting, stock control and order processing. The ASP will also be able to install the necessary technology and provide upgrades and add-ons for it when this is necessary. The advantage of an ASP is that it enables you to get applications which fit your business exactly, but there are drawbacks. The main disadvantage is that the ASP market is not as well established as the ISP sector, where you are able to choose from a number of well-established and stable names. The ASP sector has suffered a fairly high failure rate although it is worth remembering that the ISP sector – in particular where small ISPs are concerned – continues to have its share of failures. What some businesses might consider to be a further disadvantage is that the ASP has control over elements of your security. (Some businesses may see this as an advantage.) In choosing an ASP you therefore need to be very confident that their security (and other important areas such as data back-up and recovery) are as water tight as you want them to be.

ISPs

In making your choice of ISP there are a number of key considerations, including how reliable they are and what sort of traffic they can cope with and whether they will accept a commercial site (not all ISPs do). You can check on the reliability of various ISPs by using publications such as **Internet.works** which regularly carries comparisons of service providers. There are actually thousands of ISPs so you will have a very wide choice and will need to choose one very carefully. You will need to know how efficient it is, including its problem-solving and advice services, and how secure it is. Does it support encryption, firewall protection, employee security passwords and user identities should you need them?

Some Internet providers provide a free service (actually paid for by advertising that they carry). This may be completely free (a free phone connection number and free use of the service) or partially free (a local rate call and free use of the service). Telecoms providers are also likely to provide various deals for Internet connection, and these may be linked to you using them as your ISP. There are also fixed rate Internet providers where you pay a fee for unlimited monthly or annual access, although these often come with their own set of problems such as cutting you off after an hour or two hours of connection time. Fixed-rate services of this nature are unlikely to encourage commercial concerns which may need to be connected for much longer periods, or even permanently.

Questions to ask

The sort of questions which you need to ask of your ISP are how reliable it is, how secure it is, whether it is connected directly to the backbone, what types of connection it can support, whether it is a backbone provider (see below), whether there are additional features (or additional costs) which you should be aware of, and how fast it is, i.e. what sort of bandwidth will it support.

You want at least 95 per cent reliability from your provider – many boast a much better record than this. The easiest way to lose a sale (and even your reputation) is to be saddled with an ISP that cannot guarantee connections. In terms of security you want the ISP to provide firewall protection and automatic encryption to try to stop problems happening on your site. Hacking is nowhere near as big or widespread a problem as press reports would have us believe. It is just that if a teenager breaks into the Pentagon then this becomes a high-profile crime. Some ISPs offer two levels of security, a basic level and a Value Added Network (VAN) which is more secure. You will need to decide what is appropriate for your needs.

The backbone

The Internet has a 'backbone' – a main or trunk route running through it – and a number of ribs or offshoots. The most reliable and fastest providers are those that are connected directly to the backbone – these will advertise themselves as 'backbone providers'. Allocation of web space may be just as important as the connection, although most web hosts actually make more than enough space available for their clients. You may need as much as 50 Mb (which some providers will be happy to offer). Avoid providers who offer 5 Mb or less.

You may need the additional features which an ISP makes available such as, for example, domain hosting or design or transaction services for your web site. Hosts may want you to use their domain name rather than your own, but this does not always make good business sense (see page 47). You may also find that your provider places a limit on the number of pages you can have, the number of products you can sell or the number of transactions you can make in any one time period.

Establishing a presence

Your first priority will be to ensure that you have fast, clear, reliable e-mail connections for yourself and any of your partners or employees, so that the staff can contact suppliers, customers and partners and suppliers, customers and partners can contact your staff. Already you are on the way to defining a professional online presence with each employee having their own e-mail address. Your staff will each need a new business card with both your web address and their personal e-mail address on it. This may sound extravagant but, apart from being a good way of helping to get your staff on board (see Chapter 15, regarding the management of change) it also helps to publicize your business. As outlined in the previous chapter on marketing, you should order new stationery and make sure that you put your web address on it and on all your correspondence. Try to make it as prominent as space and good design will allow and, where space allows, try to let the reader know what they might find there.

Your ISP will also provide the service of logging each visitor to your site, and they will also be able to tell you at what point the visitor left the site. By doing an analysis of this information – how many times, for example, does a visitor turn into a buyer, or at what point do those visitors who don't turn into customers generally leave the site – you should be able to make your operation more effective. You can add a counter to your site to see for yourself how much traffic is being generated by going to **www.thecounter.com** and downloading one.

Reducing the risk

In the same way that you have chosen a unique and catchy name for your business (and some businesses will spend a great deal of time and money over this), you will need to create a unique web identity for yourself. You may want to trade on your existing reputation and use the same name as your existing business. This has all the advantages of carrying your image and customer loyalty over with you. It also has the disadvantage that, should your e-commerce arm fail to perform for any reason, you will have poisoned your existing good reputation. Sometimes it may be a good idea to set up a separate company from your real business – you can use the same name but just add 'trading' or 'web based' or even 'dot.com' to the title. This may mean having to produce a separate set of accounts but this is probably a good thing so that it is clear to you how well your web-based business is doing. It is also a way which allows you to trade on your established name and reputation and yet not put it at risk. You may think that this is unnecessary and that there will be no risk to the reputation of your existing business, but this is a decision that only you can take.

Domain names

Your first step in forging a web identity has to be to establish your own unique web address in a format that people can understand. You will already have a unique web address in a format that other computers can understand which is expressed, in computer terms, as a series of digits which no one but another computer will remember long enough to even write down, let alone visit your web site. These digits are usually replaced by a name, known as a domain name. What you want is a name that will trip off the tongue, identify your business and encourage people to visit your web site – all in one easy-to-remember word or short phrase. You could use the domain of your ISP, but this can often lead to a clumsy and unattractive address in the format of mybusiness@myisp.com. This is actually promoting two businesses at the same time (yours and the ISP) and therefore, in terms of publicity, recognition and brand awareness, this weakens the impact of your name. Because of the shortage of generic top-level domain names (gTLDs) the industry has decided to introduce a number of new ones in order to increase the number of naming possibilities. The original gTLDs were fairly limiting and included .org, for organizations, .ac for academic or educational sites, .co. followed by the country's initials for those businesses that wanted to be associated with a particular country or area, .net for net-based businesses and .com meaning a commercial concern. These were fairly rapidly overloaded and the industry has recognized that there is a need for a whole new set of suffixes or extensions (see below).

Risks

Unknown to many businesses on the web (particularly to many new businesses) is the fact that the failure rate of small ISPs is actually quite high – around 100 every year. Not far behind this figure are the domain name providers who are failing at the rate of around 50 every year – approximately one every week. Some of these are fairly unscrupulous operations who may have been using special offers and reduced rate name registration to get your business but, in some cases, have not even have bothered to register your name. If your domain name provider or your ISP goes out of business they are hardly likely to contact you to let you know. So you could find that, even though you may have paid for two or even five years' worth of domain name, your domain name is no longer your domain name and you need to re-register quickly before someone else does. You should check fairly regularly at **www.nominet.co.uk** for UK-based names to see if your domain name provider has registered your name and to see if you are still listed.

All the best names have gone

In November 2000, the Internet Corporation for Assigned Names and Numbers (ICANN) created seven new top-level domains which included .biz for businesses, .pro for professional organizations and specialist names such as .museum (you have to actually prove that you are a museum in order to register this one). The following year other new extensions have also been introduced. These include .shop, .sport, .club, .travel, .mp3, .kids,

'No, you can't have John, that's gone. William's gone too, and Eric – what about Thor?'

.chat, .game, .law and .ltd amongst others, making it now possible not only to have the name that you want but also an extension that says something about your business. (Visit **www.net-names.com** for further details of the current position.) In choosing a name – certainly before the new extensions came on stream – a business would often find that both its name and any reasonable variations on it had been snapped up, usually by someone in the same market as them. The new extensions mean that you are much more likely to be able to establish the identity that you want. In choosing a name you should think about what the name says about your business and your product. Some names are very good at getting the message across – **letsbuyit.com** says almost all that it needs to say in the name. On the other hand, **boo.com** (failed) and **Amazon.com** (still hanging in there but yet to make a profit) say nothing about the business. Amazon has, however, succeeded in growing the name as an established brand so that everyone recognizes it as *the* online book store. As a purely Internet-based business, it had no reputation or name to trade on so would have to have built an identity whatever name was chosen for the business. Another example is the New Zealand based 'healthy living' business called Alberon. **Alberon.com** had no 'physical' business on whose reputation it could build and is named after a street where the directors first met and shared ideas. However, the use of the 'Look Good – Feel Good' tag, the web and stationery colour scheme and the link to the purity of New Zealand products are all helping it on the way to creating a brand presence. In this case a name which 'said' something was unnecessary. **ClickMango.com** was so successful at promoting its business name (rather than its business) that the name has become more of an asset than the business behind it. Sometimes having a name which says nothing is a good thing so that if you want to expand in new directions, you can do so without being constrained by a name (furniture.com could hardly sell anything else after all). It is important to balance the need to tell your customers something about you against a need to not be constrained.

Once you have chosen the name that you would like you can visit any of the net name providers in order to see if you can register the name. If successful, there will be a fee to be paid – this varies but tends to be in the $100 to $150 mark, depending on the domain name provider, the extension that you choose and the length of time that you register the name for. The name is only yours for as long as it remains registered so, if you only register for an initial year or two (a good idea so that you can test out the strength of your business) you will have to make sure that you remember to re-register the name. The domain name provider should tell you if the name which you want is available (you should even be able to find out who has it if it's not) and be able to register it for you. You can check with **www.whois.org** and **www.easyspace.com** to see who has the name that you want. If it isn't available then try combinations, such as mybusinessonline or mybusinessplus. A good domain name provider will suggest various combinations based on the name that you initially submit.

If you have a name or brand identity that you really want to protect then you may have to take the step of registering it in more than one domain. The fact that you have mybusiness.com or mybusiness.net does not stop someone else registering the same name as, for example, mybusiness.co.uk. You may also want to register possible variations on your name. For example, **www.you4me.com** may be a successful web site selling valentine cards and associated gifts but will, sensibly, have also registered **me4you.com** as well as **you4me.org**, **you4me.net** and so on. Major players like Coca-Cola and MGM will have registered many different variations.

If you have a brand or name that is well known then you may also find that someone has bought the domain name or names that you want with the sole intention of selling it to you at a profit. There have been a number of high-profile cases regarding this so-called 'cyber sitting' and the courts have tended to come down on the side of the genuine 'owner' of the name rather than the cyber-sitter although, in some cases, there is good reason for someone else to have the name. (McDonalds could hardly stop every McDonald in the world from having a web site!) Domain names are considered as part of the intellectual property of a business and therefore part of its trade mark. They are thus protected by trade mark laws, although these will change from one country to another.

! Hints and tips!

One solution to cyber-sitting is just to change your name or domain extension, or to come up with an imaginative alternative name. You can, for example, try clever combinations of words and numbers or even text messaging (SMS) shorthand, e.g. spk2me, Ilvu etc.

? Did you know?

Networks may be intranets or extranets. An intranet is a closed network of machines connected together either directly or via telecommunications equipment. Even though the Internet can usually be accessed from it, it is 'closed' and therefore secure. An extranet is an intranet running on the Internet – the machines are connected together via private secure connections over the web. Distance is no object to some of these connections so that they can become WANs, or Wide Area Networks.

Web links

Government help for e-commerce starters can be found at **www.ukonlineforbusiness.gov.uk** in the UK. and at **www.sba.gov** in the USA. At **www.thecounter.com** you can download a web counter for your site, so that you can monitor the number of visitors to it.

You can find information regarding new extensions at **www.net-names.com**. Try **www.whois.org** and **www.easyspace.com** to see who has the name that you want.

Glossary

Business

brand identity   recognition of a business through a name, colour scheme, logo, tag line etc.

trade mark   a sign or name belonging to a business and protected in law

Information Technology

ASP   Application Service Providers are similar to ISPs except that they tend to concentrate on the business side of the net

cyber-sitting   when someone buys a domain name with the intention either of preventing someone else from using it or of selling it for a profit

e-mall   an electronic shop front where you can open a 'stall'

extranet   a private network running over the Internet

hub   the centre to which network devices can be connected

ICANN   Internet Corporation for Assigned Names and Numbers

LAN   local area network

router   sends and receives data for your network

VAN   Value Added Network with higher levels of security provided by an ISP

WAN   Wide Area Network

Summary

- You may need different levels or types of connectivity depending on the size of your organization, its structure and your intended levels of business.
- You will need to decide carefully exactly what you need for your e-commerce operation.
- An electronic shop front may be all that you need to begin with.
- Decide whether you want an ISP or an ASP, and then choose one carefully, checking costs, features and restrictions.
- You will need a domain name – choose one that reflects your current business and reputation or one that you can build as a brand; if it's catchy, all the better!
- Be careful who you register the domain name with and check regularly that it is still registered.
- If you have problems registering the name you want – be imaginative!

11 | **DESIGNING A WEBSITE**

'I thought I'd made the right decision!'

This chapter looks at the basic concepts behind good web design and at how you can transfer your physical businesses image and reputation to an e-commerce operation.

Initial decisions

You will need to first think about the primary purpose of your web site before deciding on the look of it. So, before considering the design of your web site, you need to decide what it is that you want it to do. Is its primary purpose to attract and entertain the casual visitor? Is it intended to show that you have mastered a web authoring program and can brandish your technical wizardry on the Internet? Is it to show the goods or service you are offering for sale in the best possible light? Don't imagine that you can manage to do all three simultaneously. As a commercial site its primary function is, of course, to attract as many potential customers as possible, get them to stay and buy something and then get them to return on a second and subsequent occasions – but how are you going to achieve this? If you try to achieve more than a single objective, your web site will end up looking an amateurish mess – and there is nothing worse than an unattractive site (apart from an unattractive site that takes an age to load) – which fails to fulfil any of its intended functions. The focus of your web site will depend to a great extent on the nature of your business and on the brand image you want to present.

Brand image

Not only brands but brand images are protected by trade mark laws. Coca-Cola produces bottles of a very distinctive shape and cans and labels designed using a special Coca-Cola type face and a unique and recognizable colour scheme. When this design was copied – albeit with some slight modifications – by the Sainsbury's supermarket group in the UK and used on their own brand of cola, Coca-Cola took them to court. The court ruled that the design on the Sainsbury's cola cans was indeed, based on Coca-Cola's own designs and that the cans were too similar in design, thus leading to confusion amongst customers and a diminution of the impact of the Coca-Cola brand. The supermarket cans threatened the brand by threatening its brand image.

There is a lot more to establishing a brand image, however, than just the design of a label or a can. Branding is used to give a particular value or image to a product. Successful branding means that new products can be launched bearing the brand name and consumers will assume that they have the same brand values as the existing products. This can be used to the advantage of an existing business with a good brand image. The web-based side of such a business would immediately benefit from an established good name provided the web site was a good one. And this is a big proviso – it has to include all of the aspects of the e-commerce part of the business, not just the web site, but the web site is perhaps the most important part, being the 'point of entry' for the customer. It is in effect, the shop front for the business. Most brands cultivate a particular image, closely linked to the range of products that they produce. The image of the Virgin Group, for example, is centred around its chairman and founder Richard Branson. The product image is one of value for money, quality, adventurousness and innovation. For Nike the image is one of exclusivity, originality and success. For the Body Shop the image is of being environmentally friendly and of selling fairly traded goods, while Heinz conveys family values, value for money and quality ingredients. Visit the site of **Alberon.com** and you will immediately see that its image is one of green credentials, natural products and health. The colour scheme, the images used, the tag line, the use of the native New Zealand koru fern – all combine successfully to give this image.

Halo effect

A strong brand image can promote sales throughout a product range – this is known as the halo effect. For example, the Nike brand is now used on many items that are not sportswear and therefore a long way from its core business. They still sell, however, because they carry the Nike values. The halo effect makes it much easier to launch and establish new products. If you think of your web site as a new product this might help you to focus on what you need to do to make it a success. Don't forget, if you cause damage to your reputation through a poorly constructed web site or through badly operated e-commerce, this will have a detrimental knock-on effect on your existing business. Damage to a brand image can have far-reaching consequences. Coca-Cola's European operation was damaged in the late 1990s by a scare involving bottling plants in Belgium. Although there was no danger to the public and the company took the correct steps to both protect and inform its customers, the image of the company was tarnished. Similarly when Mercedes Benz had problems with their 'Baby Benz' (it tended to fall over when cornering) this reflected badly on the image of the company as a whole.

Focus

Your first task is to decide what the main focus of your web site is going to be, and the second is to work out how you are going to either incorporate or create a brand image. Your web site will look very different depending on which of the three aims – attracting and entertaining visitors, showing your technical wizardry or showing your product in the best light – is your primary focus. Consider which emphasis will be best for your business, rather than any other reason.

The first possible aim is to attract and entertain visitors. On the whole, web users visit specific sites to be entertained. These sites will feature strongly in their personal preference and bookmark lists and links. You are not likely to be one of them unless you are catering to a specific sector of this particular market, in which case the nature of the service that you are providing will mean that this must be the primary focus of your web site. You may, for example, be providing online film reviews of the latest releases, in which case, you can attract this particular clientele. But remember, they have visited your site to read the reviews – and they don't want to take forever to find them. People who came to the Internet and e-commerce early will remember it as being a medium which was much more text based than image based. Now, however, most machines are fast enough to download graphics, photographs and even moving pictures. Design has consequently moved much more towards colour and images rather than text. In the case of reviews (or similar), however, the primary focus will be the text and so there is little point in having much else. The image of the site can still be created by using promotional stills from films (with permission) or by the appropriate 'backdrop' to each page on the site, but it is the text – and its readability – that is going to be the most important element.

If your aim is to show your technical wizardry on the net, you need to consider whether this is appropriate to the nature of the product that you are dealing in. If your e-commerce business requires you to demonstrate that you can make frames do back flips, or lettering fly in on a golden cloud, or have the ability to morph words into pictures and back again then, by all means demonstrate that you can do so. Perhaps your e-commerce business is offering to build web sites for other businesses, in which case skills and techniques such as these may need to be emphasized. (Otherwise, it is unlikely that they will do a great deal other than annoy!) It is still true to say that if the site takes an age to load, you will lose many customers before they have even seen the site. Many web designers have come into the web from other design routes and, in particular, you will see the influence of newspaper and magazine designs on many pages. The principles of such design – clarity, crispness and impact – are the sort of principles which need to be transferred on to the web when you design your own pages.

Finally, your aim may be to show a product in the best possible light. How you manage to do this will depend on whether you are selling goods or a service. If you are selling a service – and the intention is to get people to visit the site and then contact you directly – then you should include testimonials or other recommendations as well as examples of successfully completed work. A garden designer, for example, could post photographs of completed gardens and comments from satisfied customers. Additional extras are always welcome – in this case, for example, there could be a link to a plant sales site, or a page on common garden design problems and how to solve them. If you are selling a product then getting people to stay may be achieved through photographs, descriptions, or technical information on your range. You should emphasize what it will do, how well it will do it and, perhaps most importantly, what its main features are. You will need to point out what makes it different to the competition. However, you will still need to avoid the pitfalls described below, such as slow-loading pages due to an excess of photographs. You will need to strike a balance between what is necessary to describe and promote your product fully and what is desirable in terms of loading time. If you are using an outsource, then you need to be sure that it is one that will not produce either a 'whistles and bells' site or a dull one.

Brand creation

If you have a brand image or reputation, it is going to give you a head start over the competition if you can carry this over to your web site. You should be using the same colour schemes, the same logos, the same catch phrases and tag lines that you use in your existing business. If you are looking to create a brand online, then go about it in the same way that you would create any other brand image. Decide on the image that you want your product to project and then reinforce that image with whatever tools are to hand. This means that your advertising should only be in those journals and magazines that reflect your image, promotions should always reinforce your image and public relations can be used to both establish the image and to spread it. If you can establish a solid brand reputation then you are a long way to ensuring that your business is a success.

Keeping the customer

Assuming that a prospective customer has gone to the trouble of tracking down your site, you must then decide, firstly, what you would like them to do and, secondly, how you are going to persuade them to do it. A third consideration is to try to keep them from leaving your site accidentally – links to other sites can, for example, mean that prospective buyers go and never come back. Once they are off on a different track (and it may even be a vital advertiser's hyper-link that takes them there), they may forget what it was that they set out to do in the first place. The web is, increasingly, a tool for the moment. Attention spans might easily and accurately be compared to the attention span of a goldfish which, apparently, fails to get bored out of its tiny goldfish skull because it can't concentrate for long enough to recognize that it's been round this bowl before. Web users can thus light on a site, find it interesting, find an interesting-looking link on it – and be gone before you have had time to engage them with your brilliant ideas and arguments. Sometimes, even if they want to get back, it is a task which is beyond their capabilities.

The first thing to decide is on the priorities for your customers. Would you like them to be impressed by your business's corporate or brand identity? If so, you may need to colour the site in your distinctive shades or to make a feature of a logo, and to cut down the amount of text on the homepage to a minimum. If, however, there is a lot of information on your site and a large number of different places to visit, you should be trying to emphasize clarity in the layout and to make navigation as easy as possible. In almost all cases, the 'with bells on' approach of moving images, sound and animations, pop-ups and reveals serve to do little other than increase download time and cause annoyance to the prospective customer. Think about your own attitude on entering a shop – if the shopkeeper made you wait in the doorway whilst they played you a jingle and then provided you with a maze to solve before entering a badly laid-out store, you would probably not buy anything and would certainly be put off returning!

If the site contains a lot of graphics and moving images it will take a long time to download. The Internet is probably best at the art of the instant; many people browsing (don't be fooled by the relaxed sounding nature of the word) the Internet will be put off by anything that takes above 20 seconds to load.

Typeface choices

Many sites also suffer from over design. They rely on many colours and font types to put what they think is a clear and powerful message across, in much the same way that a 'comic book' does. If, however, you need a cooler, more professional approach (to be recommended) you need to take your cue from the designers of company logos and corporate identity packages. These are usually clear and concise. Even daily newspapers can provide a clue to effective design. They will use only a few font types (although they may vary the size and style, using italics and emboldening) and these are likely to be clear and readable. It is no accident that most reading matter is not printed in swirly 'handwriting' fonts like *handscript* or special effects type fonts like horror – the sort of typefaces that make text decidedly difficult to read.

You should choose a couple of font types that go together, are easily readable, and which, if possible, reflect the character of your site. This book is typeset in 11 point Times – a serif font which has clear lines and excellent readability. Times New Roman has the 'serif' or little tails that characterize the letters, but is still clear and readable. Either can be rendered as bold, italic, in different sizes, with shadows or in different colours, whilst still maintaining the generic look that will come by using a limited font range. Some fonts may be particularly suitable for your product or service – fonts such as this can be attractive for kids – *or this one for a more informal approach*. But remember, readability is the key.

The other thing to be careful of is colour combinations. If you put a dark font on a dark background then it is likely to vanish. Some colour combinations are excellent and work well – these are called complementary colours on the colour wheel (such as red and green, yellow and blue) and each colour, when used with its partner, actually makes the other colour look brighter.

Ease of navigation

A good site needs to be clear and readable as a first priority. While this is a necessary condition, it is not however a sufficient condition to make a good web site. It is possible to produce a web site that fulfils all these conditions – it is clear, easy to understand, easy to read and loads quickly – and yet still have difficulties in navigating the site. For example, hyper-links within the site may not be obvious or may not take the prospective customer to where they thought they were going. Because there are various different ways on the web in which to achieve the same effect, all sites will be unique. What you have to do is to bury at least some of those urges to do things in an exciting and innovative way and borrow methods from sites where you have found them to be effective. Visit other sites, look at what works and what doesn't work. See what you find easy to cope with. Better still, introduce a net virgin friend or relation to some sites and see where they encounter difficulties of understanding or navigation. Before the site goes 'live' you could set up your own personal focus group. Let a small group of friends, colleagues and family have a look at the web site and see what they think of it – you don't have to take their advice, but you should listen to it.

What keeps them coming back?

Figure 8

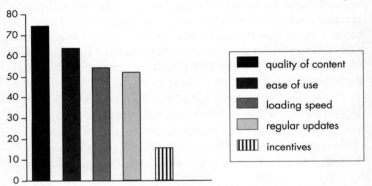

What customers found were the most important factors in bringing them back to a site

The bar chart shows what one researcher found to be the major factors influencing whether a visitor returned to a web site for a second or subsequent visit. Perhaps surprisingly, promotional offers giving something away were the least attractive feature. This is possibly because the average web user has a certain amount of marketing savvy and can see through the promotional offers, many of which are just designed to tie you into future purchases or commitments. The most important factor is the quality of the content – this means both the actual content and the way in which it has been presented – with 75 per cent of the survey respondents rating this above anything else. Next, with 66 per cent, came the ease with which a surfer could navigate round the site and get to where they wanted; this would also be linked to the next most important factor cited, which is the download speed. Over half also thought that the regularity and usefulness of updates was an important factor.

There are three main things you should aim to incorporate into your design. These are efficiency, utility and clarity. Your site should handle transactions quickly, easily and painlessly. It should attract customers, keep their attention and make sure that they return. It is important that it is providing a service – remember why customers go back to a particular business and how a successful business succeeds in locking you in. You should also make sure that your site adds value – how many people swear by 'their' hairdresser or 'their' favourite restaurant just because they are made to feel that little bit special there? Customers should return to your web site as 'old friends'. For example, if they make a purchase, this should be the only time that they have to enter details. On subsequent visits, your site should recognize them and welcome them like an old friend – this added value is often the dividing line between a successful web site and a failed one.

Web links

To find out more about web design, try **www.webpagesthatsuck.com**, a site that tries to show how badly sites can be designed by criticizing poorly designed sites – often the sites of big businesses. For design advice aimed at all levels of web designer go to **www.webreference.com**

Did you know?

A 'pop-up' is usually an advertisement or link to another site that will appear in front of the page that you are loading. Some are even clever enough to take you to another web site if you try to delete them. On commercial sites customers tend to find them annoying and off-putting – a bit like the hard sell in the real world.

! **Hints and tips!**
You should always use your existing logos, colours, lettering and catch phrases to maintain a strong link between the web business and your existing business. In this way your web business can feed off the success of your existing business. If you are a pure e-commerce start-up, you should try to develop and establish a brand image.

Glossary

Business

corporate identity   the way a company or business projects its image, through devices such as company colours, uniforms, use of standard fonts, standard designs etc – just look round in your local supermarket to see this at work

brand   a word/words or symbol, rendered in a specific way, that identifies that this product is made by this business, e.g. Johnnie Walker for a particular Scotch whisky

halo effect   the way a good brand can promote sales of other products

logo   the symbol that represents the business; there are some very powerful ones, e.g. the Nike tick, the Unilever 'U', the Johnnie Walker 'man with walking stick'

Information Technology

italic   fonts that are rendered so that they slope – *like this*

bold   fonts that are rendered so that they are dark – **like this**

hyper-links   'buttons' that take a user directly to another page

font   the computer term for a typeface; a style of lettering

navigating   finding your way around a web site

web site   a collection of pages, linked together to form a coherent whole

Summary

- There are certain points that should be uppermost in your mind when thinking of creating a web site:
  - purpose – why is the site being created?
  - clientele – who are you aiming to attract to the site?
  - design – how is the design going to help your product or service to sell?
  - clarity – how do you make sure that your site is clearly readable and easily navigable?
- You need to strike a balance between clear but dull and over-designed 'bells and whistles' – either extreme will put customers off.
- It is important to transfer your existing successful brand image to the site by using design to give it a brand identity.
- Research shows that quality of content, ease of use and download speed are all cited as being more important than special offers.

12 WRITING AND LAUNCHING A WEB SITE

'I wish I'd not taken this on myself...'

To try or not to try?

Your first decision must be whether you decide to take on this task yourself or to employ someone to do it for you. There are advantages and disadvantages to both courses of action. Doing the job yourself probably means embarking on a programme of self-education – and one with a fairly steep learning curve. If you have a background or other experience in print design – leaflets, newsletters or other publications – you may find the design part easier but will still have to learn the technical stuff. This means a commitment in time which your business may not be able to afford. However, it does mean that you will never be short of the expertise that you need. It is also, initially, the least costly way to start. Bringing in an expert means that you will have to choose one, pay for one, brief one and trust one. If any of these essentials is missed out, the hiring of an expert could cost you more than you bargained for. This is also likely to be the more expensive option, but possibly the faster one if you are keen to be up and running. Choosing an 'expert' should be undertaken with some care. Personal recommendation is the best sort of advertisement and you should also be able to see other work which the designer has completed. The service might be expensive but the designer actually has no initial costs except time. This means that there is no need to make any payments before the site is completed. Anyone who asks for large sums 'up front' giving the excuse that they will have a lot of equipment to buy is obviously not properly geared up to provide you with a service and should not be taken on. You must make sure that you have a clear idea of what you actually want on the site, and how you want it to look, and you must communicate this to the designer very clearly. You should be able to see the 'work in progress' and be aware if it is going outside of your requirements or 'vision'. Finally, you will need to trust your designer; you can't oversee every little part of the design and may have to leave certain decisions to his or her professional good sense. If you have made a good choice then this will not be a problem. Buying in the necessary design and technical skills does mean that you will not have the expertise in-house and will need to buy in on a regular basis for updates and other changes. If this is the case, you might want to think about outsourcing the whole e-commerce operation to an expert or agency as this might be cheaper in the long run. They would sort out connections and communications, design, author and launch your web site, and maintain and update it as necessary. The biggest disadvantage of this, of course, is that you would lose a certain amount of control over the operation.

If you are not confident then there are many ways in which you can practise, without the site actually going up for anyone else to see. If you have decided that you either don't have the skills or (more likely) don't have the time for the enterprise, then there are a number of ways in which you can proceed. You can hire a professional, use an e-mall hosting service or go to web site builders such as **http://webstop.virtualave.net** who will design your web site for you (usually within a month). While there is no charge for this service, Webstop will require you to host a banner advertising them on your site.

If you are going to do it yourself, you will need to devote some time to familiarizing yourself with the various web-building, hosting, launching and so forth options. It is advisable to start with something reasonably simple and then, when you have mastered that, move forward. The sense of achievement at completing your first web site will make the work that has gone into it well worthwhile. You could try building a family oriented or hobby site first before moving on to anything that you would wish your customers to see. The ISP which you use to access the Internet will have provided you with a certain amount of web space and you should have access to web page building tools from your browser.

One way to stay in touch with scattered elements of family and friends around the world is to set up a web site and this could be your first project. As with your commercial web site you must start by planning carefully what is to appear where. You will need to decide on the number of pages that you initially want (although this can be changed later) and the basic look of your site. You will need to make sure that you have assembled all of the relevant hardware and software for your site as well as any images or effects that you wish to include. Do you, for example, need photo manipulation software? Do you have the facility to transfer photographs or other images to your site? Do you have the software required to write your page and to submit it to your ISP? If you have all the necessary things in place for a personal web site, then you can begin to build it.

DIY

Pages are written in the universal programming language of the web called Hyper Text Mark-up Language, or HTML. You will be relieved to know that you do not have to learn HTML straight away – you can get away without learning it at all, but if you are going to develop your skills, you will need to cross this bridge at some point. It is not a difficult language to learn (of course, it comes naturally to programmers) and there are sites where you can get assistance in the form of tutorials. For example **http://html.digitalsea.net** offers seven fairly straightforward steps to learning HTML. HTML is not a complicated language – as computer languages go – and it is likely that you will fairly quickly become familiar with it. But you do not have to learn the language in order to get yourself started. A number of popular web site building packages will accept your version of how you want your site to look and write the code for you. You must know exactly how you want each page to look, however, as usually it is a wysiwyg sytem – what you see is what you get.

Tools and freebies

Before entering into the realm of HTML you can build a good and adequate (if not exciting) site using tools which are provided free with your browser if you use Netscape Navigator or may be present if you have the correct version of Microsoft Internet Explorer. There are also professional packages (which can still be learned fairly easily by the dedicated amateur) which include HotMetal (approximately $300), Microsoft FrontPage (approximately $150), Dreamweaver and CoffeeCup (each approximately $300). The cut-down version of Microsoft FrontPage, called FrontPage Express, used to be available free through Internet Explorer 4. This had the advantage of being simple to use and not requiring a knowledge of HTML as the program writes the code for you. If you have a later version of Internet Explorer, however, you will find that the software is no longer there. Microsoft have decided to withdraw it and so it is not only no longer available, but also all reference, support and the possibility of downloading it from the Microsoft site have been removed. It can still be obtained, however (see Did You Know? on page 183). Netscape also has its own web editor called Netscape Composer, which also does not require a knowledge of HTML and is provided with templates and a 'wizard'.

FrontPage Express is, as you would expect, Microsoft-centric – but if you are familiar with MS applications this will be a big advantage, as you can plan and write your test pages on a word processor and then transfer this to the web writing software.

Netscape with Navigator, and Microsoft with Internet Explorer are, of course, rivals. This can mean that a site constructed with one particular application may struggle to look right if viewed in the rival one. It is often a good idea to add a rider to the site somewhere to say that 'this site is best viewed in Netscape Navigator' or 'best viewed in Internet Explorer', depending on which one it has been constructed under and how it behaves with the other one. The problems that arise can be to do with how colours are presented – your wonderful background might look gloomy and grey through its rivals window – and in how pictures are dealt with. Some, created in one version, may be very slow to load or fail to load at all when presented via the rival.

Looking at Netscape Composer as an example (as it is still generally available), this allows you to build a simple web site. You will need to be a member of the Netscape community (membership is free), and can then log onto Netscape's 'site central'. From this site you can use either Netscape Composer or Site Maker to build your page, starting from scratch or from one of the templates (with a limited range of clipart and photographs) which are provided. The site also provides for you to launch your site onto the Netscape home area. If you want to launch your site with its own domain name, you can still create it using the same software and then use a File Transfer Protocol to send it to the host that you have chosen.

Most ISPs also provide web-authoring software along with the web space. These may also, however, be membership sites that will cost you to join. Two of the biggest ones (and therefore well established and reliable) are at Compuserve and AOL (America online).

Structure

The first page that most people will see is your home page – the page that tells visitors quickly and clearly what you are about and provides them with links to all of your other pages. Whilst it is usually possible for people to enter your site through a 'back door' and thus avoid your home page, nine out of ten visitors will actually enter this way. Your home page is thus like the front cover of a magazine. Think about what appears on the front cover of a magazine that makes you want to buy it; after all, it is only the front cover that you can see on the newsagent's stand, so it must be this that has attracted you to buy. A magazine will have an attractive cover that will provide a big clue as to what is inside: a bike magazine will have a bike on the front, a running magazine a runner, a fashion magazine a model; it will also have 'teasers' enticing you to look inside – these are short phrases that are designed to arouse your interest. It will also have the contents and special flashes for anything that the editor thinks is special or crucial to sales. Your home page must try to fulfil the same function. It should immediately identify your business (if you can do this through a recognized logo or colour scheme this is better – and faster loading – than a photograph) so that searchers know that they have hit on the right page. If you have had stationery professionally printed then your printer will have a copy of your logo on disc. The 'contents' should all be hyper-links to other pages, and should contain 'teasers' to get you to delve further. It can also show (for regular visitors) what is new by using 'new' flashes. You don't have to use text for your links. 'Buttons' can be downloaded from a number of outlets – just search the web with the phrase 'applet button factory'.

You do have one advantage over the magazine publisher in that you can provide movement on your page. Animated banners and other dynamic effects can easily be incorporated (visit **http//:webservices.adobe.com/banner/main.html** to create dynamic banners) but be wary of doing too much as you don't want a slow download speed. The magazine publisher has the advantage that his entire page can be taken in in one glance.

Artwork, photographs and moving images

You can put drawing files, icons and other images such as photographs on to your site by either creating them or importing them from the Internet or from CD collections. Images can be edited, enlarged and enhanced in a photo manipulation software package such as Photoshop. Animations can be created quite easily; many icons and common signs (such as pointing hands) are available in online image libraries. Remember, however, that the more complicated the image, the longer it will take to download. Images should normally be saved as JPEGs or GIFs to make it easier for web technology to handle them. (JPEG's, GIFs and TIFFs are the most common file type for saving pictures.)

If you are going to produce your own pictures of your products to be displayed on the web site (recommended), then you will need either a scanner or digital camera. The latter option of these two is better – with the former you will be relying on the quality of the photographs scanned and on the scanner itself and the process will be a lot slower. With a camera you will be able to take as many shots as you want (you just delete the ones you don't want) and can download them directly into your computer. Quality can be further enhanced by using photo-editing software to cut, frame or otherwise manipulate images. The photo editor is an important piece of kit for keeping a site crisp. Each photograph on the site will have two versions – a smaller, lower resolution image that gives customers an idea of the product, which is linked to the larger, full image. The small version should be created in your photo-editing software at a much lower resolution and then rendered as a link to the original, clear version. In this way, linking what is called a 'thumbnail' with a larger and better defined image, you can keep your site's ability to load quickly and still provide quality product images for customers.

In most authoring software, creating a hyper-link is no more than saying which 'object' (text, button, image etc.) is to be rendered as a link, and what it is to link to. Most versions of authoring software know exactly what the main features are that web authors will require, and make it easy for even the novice to achieve the desired effect.

Hosting a domain name

If you have decided that you would like your own domain (again, recommended) then you will need a web host. Some of these will charge you for hosting, but not all. Free domain hosts include **www.freeweb.com** and **www.webprovider.com**. Once you have created your site (and saved it all into a single directory folder on your hard drive) you will need to transfer the files on your web site to the web host. This will require a small piece of software called a file transfer protocol or FTP. There are a number of these around, some of which are free. CuteFTP can be found at **www.cuteFTP.com** (costs $40) while others include FTP Express at **www.intellisys.mn.com**, (costs $24.95) or CupertinoFTP at **http//:members.xoom.com/cupertinoFTP** (free).

Once you have uploaded your site, visit it and test that it is all working. At this stage it may be open to public scrutiny, but no one except you actually knows that it is there, so it is unlikely to come in for any criticism. Only spread the word about its existence once you are sure that it is right.

Keeping it fresh

You will need to update your site at least once a month (you will have to find the time for this if you are developing the site yourself – it's worth it), otherwise the site will quickly look tired and jaded. You want people to visit more than once – ideally you want them to store a direct link to you in their 'bookmarks' (also called 'favorites' [sic]). They won't do this unless they can see that there is some 'movement' on the site – something new that might tempt them to linger a little longer or to visit again in hope of coming across something new.

Keeping your web site up to date is very important. If a customer returns to a site and there is nothing new, or if it looks like the site owner or webmaster has not done anything since the last visit, then an air of abandonment pervades the site and the customer slopes off elsewhere. The problem in keeping a site up to date is two-fold. First, there is the tactical decision of choosing what it is that can be deleted from the site; second is the time and effort that has to be put into altering the site. You will, at the least, have to go back into the software that you used to write the page. If you have used a simple (simple in that it writes the HTML code for you) program such as FrontPage Express or Netscape Composer this will not be too much of a bind. If, however, you have used a program that requires you to enter HTML, then you have to go into the code to change it.

You will get better with practice, but alternatively you can consider using what is called a web logger (or blogger). This is the web equivalent of keeping a diary. You can keep visitors apprised of current change and developments and previous entries are also available for them to read. For a commercial web site this can be used like a 'what's coming' or 'what's new in the shop' notice. 'New versions of xyz stock due in next week' can be added very quickly to the log and shows customers that there is planned movement or updating on the site. Web log sites can be created by clicking on **www.blogger.com** and following the screen-by-screen steps. You can place the log in the free area provided and provide hyper-links to and from it to your page (the easiest option) or you can put it in your own web space. Either way, you will be providing your customers and prospective customers with further information and letting them know that your site is not static.

Taking the money

How the money for commercial transactions can be collected is discussed in the next chapter. If, as an existing business, you already have the capability to take credit card payments, using something as simple as a card swipe machine, you will be able to take orders online. This is not as easy or as convenient, of course, as being able to handle transactions online automatically. It means that you have to receive the credit card number and then key it into your machine manually. This is not a problem if you are only getting half a dozen to a dozen purchases a day but, once it rises much above that, the amount of time that you will save by having a merchant account becomes significant. A merchant account will allow you to handle credit and debit card transactions and check the ability of customers to pay. There will be a price, however, so it is worth shopping round to see which bank or financial institution can offer you the best deal.

Search engines

Once your site is complete and launched, you will be wanting people to visit it. The main way to do this (apart from the publicity that you give the site through your own marketing) is to register it on a number of search engines. Below are the main search engines, the UK-centric ones identifiable by the **.co.uk** after their name. The others can be made to search particular geographical areas or in different languages. They are given in alphabetical order rather than any order of efficiency or reach. All perform much the same function although some are bigger than others.

Search Engines

www.altavista.com
www.excite.com
www.freepages.co.uk
www.google.com
www.hotbot.lycos.com
www.infoseek.go.com
www.lycos.com
www.northernlight

www.searchuk.co.uk
www.ukdirectory.co.uk
www.ukindex.co.uk
www.webcrawler.com
www.yahoo.co.uk
www.yahoo.com
www.yell.co.uk

These are the major search engines, but there are many others, local, specialist or new, that you may wish to register with. You can submit your site to the major search engines by logging on to **www.all4one.com/all4submit**. This will not cover all search engines, however (Yahoo is one of the biggest and you will need to log onto it in order to submit your web site. Look in the menus for 'submit URL' [your web address] or a similar instruction).

There are two ways of rising to the top of the search engine lists. One is to choose appropriate and effective META tags, the other is to become a popular site. The more hits you get, i.e. the more visitors, the higher up the search engine tree you will rise, so if you can encourage people to visit – even though they may not buy anything – this is good for attracting more visitors in the future. META tag keywords are the tags that are used by search engines to 'categorize' your site and should therefore be the terms that a surfer is most likely to use in looking for your product. You will also have room to place a title tag and a brief description of your pages. This should be used as another opportunity for some marketing. Usually you can have up to a thousand characters so you need to use this to give a brief outline of your business. 'My business, providing natural health products from environmentally sound sources' is much better than just 'My business'. Some search engines will show the first words of the title when a search is made, most also show the opening words of the description. For your META tags you should just enter a string of words, not separated by any punctuation, which the search engine will then use to make combinations of words. If you have a number of products which use the same word, you therefore only have to enter it once. So, for example, if you are selling health products you might have lines that include 'natural honey' 'natural beeswax' and 'natural extracts' but will only have to include the word 'natural' once. 'Natural' 'honey', 'beeswax' and 'extracts' would produce all your necessary combinations. In this case, rather than repeat 'natural' put in 'nature' to increase the possibility of being found.

In general, you will not gain any advantage by using a META tag term more than once. In fact, if you repeat the tag too many times in the hope of attracting more visitors you will actually only achieve two things – you will cut down the number of potential visitors as they will have searched on other terms which you haven't included, and at best you may be moved down the priority order of the search engine; at worst, you may be banned by them.

If you want to see how a site has entered its META tags then look at the source code on a page that you have found. This is in either Source or Page Source of the View menu depending on whether you are in Microsoft explorer or Netscape navigator.

It is also worth doing a search to see what variations of your name yield the most responses – for your web identity you need to choose the variation that yields fewer responses as this means that while your business will be found, less competition should be thrown up by the search engine. In other words, try to work out how your prospective customers will search for your product or service. Will they look for 'education resource' or 'educational resource'? Will they look for 'health food', 'health-food', 'healthfood' or even 'healthy food'? Sometimes getting a better response is as simple as having or not having a hyphen. Try looking up ebusiness and e-business, ecommerce and e-commerce. Do you think that most searchers use the hyphen or not? Check with your search engine provider to see which variation of your name is the more popular. (Perhaps surprisingly, in most cases searchers don't include the hyphen; this means that if you do, you will be missed by ... most searchers!) It is also a good idea to see what titles, descriptions and META tags have been used by your competitors. See what they have missed in their key words and also what is effective for them. What have you missed in your key words that they have included?

Golden rules

Your web site should be like a good newspaper report – simple, clear and up to date. If it is a good site, and good for the customers you wish to attract, then it will improve in popularity over time and become an integral part of your successful business strategy.

Web links

Free domain hosts include **www.freeweb.com** and **www.webprovider.com**. FTP sites include **www.cuteFTP.com**, and FTP Express at **www.intellisys.mn.com**, CupertinoFTP at **http//:members.xoom.com/cupertinoFTP**, and **www.all4one.com/all4submit** can be used to submit your site to a number of major search engines.

Did you know?

There are still copies of FrontPage Express lurking out there. If you have an older version of MS Internet Explorer you may find that you still have the software on your hard disc. Otherwise, find an older version on a magazine CD and extract the software from there (you are looking for **FPEsetup.cab**, will need to unzip all the files and save them to a new directory then double click on **fpxpress.exe** to start the installation program).

Glossary

Business

teasers   short phrases which describe stories inside a publication; meant to persuade you to buy it

Information Technology

HTML   Hyper Text Mark-up Language, the computer language of web pages

wysywyg   what you see is what you get – the software will produce a page as you see it on screen

clipart   images (usually line drawings) that can be added to documents

home page   the first page of your site, an important point which most visitors will come to first

thumbnail   a small version of a larger or better defined image

FTP   File Transfer Protocol – the way to get your site on to its host

META tags   the key words that help search engines categorize your site and searchers to find it

Summary

- Your first decision must be whether you have the time (and inclination) to construct your own site or not.
- You do not, initially, have to learn a programming language, but it will be useful later.
- The Netscape Navigator browser has built in, free web authoring software; the Microsoft version in Internet Explorer is no longer widely available.
- Sites built using some web authoring software may not reproduce well through the opposition's browser.
- Photographs and other images need to be sharp and easily transferred by scanner or digital camera.
- Web sites need to be updated regularly.
- Once launched, web sites need to be registered with search engines.
- Careful choice of key words, title and descriptions can help to make the site easier to find and more popular.

13 | KEEPING IT SECURE

There are three problems which currently haunt the cyber industry – speed, availability and security. Speed should be coped with by increased bandwidth and, like the growth in PC hard disc capacity, this is likely to be geometric. Availability – especially the notion of being always online – is coming in the form of cable and 3G access. Security problems are being dealt with very quickly, with solutions for both consumers and sellers being developed.

Whenever a high-profile 'hacking' incident is reported in the national press of a country, it rebounds badly on the confidence that consumers have in e-commerce businesses. People are often worried that their credit card numbers will fall into the wrong hands and that all they have discovered on the net is a new way of being robbed! Cyber security will not, however, be an issue for long. It is too big a stumbling block for the Internet community to ignore, and solutions are being developed at almost breakneck pace. From the business point of view, a safe and guaranteed way of collecting payment is essential. The ability to collect payments for very small transactions also opens up a lot of new possibilities.

A safer way to pay

One of the perennial problems for small businesses is collecting payment. This is magnified for small businesses on the Internet by the twin evils of uncertainty and insecurity. Combined with these is the fact that, should there be any fraud on a credit card transaction, it is the seller who is generally liable. They will have delivered a product in good faith even though it has been ordered fraudulently. While credit card companies protect their card-holders from the worst ravages of such fraud, the seller is left to shoulder the cost.

Credit card users may be worried about allowing their card details on to the web for fear that they will be revealed and used fraudulently (although the most common way for a criminal to obtain a credit card number is from a discarded supermarket receipt). Sellers need to have the reassurance that the person using the credit card number is the actual owner of the card or has the right to use it. Smart cards carrying information on microchip may be one answer in allowing customers to pay for goods online without revealing their credit card number. The system also allows sellers to confirm that the sale is genuine, thus putting both parties in a much better frame of mind when it comes to purchasing over the Internet. The scheme is being promoted by the EMV Group (whose members are Europay, Mastercard and Visa) and will make use of mobile phone technology. Newer credit cards (and eventually all credit cards) will come with a built in microchip. New generation mobile phones will have a slot into which the credit card will fit. The elements of the package are thus mobile phone (which could also be Internet enabled to make the transaction even more smooth), microchip-carrying credit card and a pin number to allow payments to be taken from the card. The system also uses text messaging (SMS – Short Messaging Service) – the mobile phone 'add-on' that was almost missed off mobile technology but which has shown such growth potential. For e-commerce transactions this would have enormous benefits in terms not only of security, but of making the process of buying so much easier. Currently, a website is likely to need information such as name and address as well as the card's details, number and expiry date. This could mean entering upwards of 80 characters (on average name and address runs to over 50 characters on its own) every time a new web site is used for a purchase. It also means that all of this personal information is floating around in the ether and making potential web buyers very nervous.

The new system involves one four-digit pin number and is thus quicker, easier and more secure. As an e-commerce provider, you advertise goods or services for sale on a web site. A potential customer decides to buy and indicates that they would like to pay using this system. Your site would then ask for (and need) just two pieces of information – the mobile phone number and the bank of the buyer. The web site then contacts the bank which forwards an SMS to the buyer's phone asking them to confirm the sale. The buyer confirms by inserting the credit card into the special slot in the phone and entering the pin number. Your site then receives confirmation of the purchase from the bank, along with the buyer's address so that you can make delivery. The whole process is thus made shorter, more efficient and yet also more secure.

Smart cards

All security issues may ultimately be resolved through the use of a smart card. Smart cards carry a chip instead of a magnetic strip, allowing them to hold enormous amounts of information. And there is no reason why the smart card should not be with you for life – unlike its two- to three-year magnetic strip cousin, it has a life span of at least forty years. The smart card is already in use in many countries and for different applications. There are two to three million in use in the UK, and they are popular in mainland Europe. Hong Kong uses them for travel (they are recognized by train, bus or even aeroplane companies). The cards are able to verify and protect identities and cannot be cloned in the way that magnetic strip cards are cloned by fraudsters. They can hold what is termed biometric information, such as fingerprints, retina patterns and voice recognition. A single swipe can verify your identity, order a product, take your address and debit your bank account in one fell swoop. How is this likely to affect e-commerce? The new generation mobile phones will all have the ability to swipe cards as well as connect to the Internet. 2.5G phones (the half-way house between mobile technology and 3G) have the capacity already. So browsing, ordering and secure payment should become amazingly simple and effective.

No more cash

Cards – especially smart cards – may actually become the only way to pay. Some major economies have been attempting to do away with currency altogether. This is not something particularly new or revolutionary, however. For example, it has been a goal of

Singapore for many years now. Countries which are ahead of the technological game have already dispensed with a lot of cash transactions. In New Zealand, for example, it is commonplace to key your pin number into a keypad for even the smallest transactions such as a beer or a cup of coffee. Many countries have seen less and less need for cash transactions which have disadvantages for governments, individuals and traders. Cash transactions are inconvenient, as cash is insecure and transactions may go unrecorded or untraced. Governments are particularly keen to cut out cash payments which make it difficult for them to collect the appropriate tax. Although certain sections of the community would want to keep cash for these very reasons, governments are unlikely to be convinced of the case and more and more transactions will be paid on a non-cash basis. In the UK, for example, the government has decided to pay state benefits directly into the recipient's bank account in an attempt to cut out the enormous amount of fraud which surrounds the current cash transactions. Benefits can end up going to the wrong person, or being intercepted, or even being claimed by the dead! To this end, the government is making sure that everyone can have an account by establishing a 'people's bank' at the post office. Benefits will be electronically (and therefore much more cheaply) credited to the account for recipients to collect. This will open up a whole new tranche of non-cash possibilities to a section of the population that currently works mostly on a cash basis.

In Britain, cash transactions still account for around 80 per cent of all purchases. Of course, the corner shop, the sandwich bar, the chippie and the pub are yet to join the card-carrying clan in any great numbers. In the USA, cards have been acceptable for many years and company cards are now beginning to take over from bank-based or Amex-type cards. The Mobil Speedpass, for example, allows customers to use not just Mobil stations, but also McDonalds, Exxon stations and numerous stores. It may be that the need to collect cash becomes less and less of a problem as such electronic advances become internationally acceptable. Singapore is pioneering a form of digital 'cash' and travellers in Hong Kong can pay for journeys (and coffee, phone calls and snacks) without the card ever having to leave their pocket.

In e-commerce terms seconds are precious – the faster the customer is able to pay for the purchase, the more likely they are to go ahead and buy. Often web sites demand inordinate amounts of information from customers – 12 digits for the credit card, 4 for the expiry date, 20 for name, 50 for the address – much of which customers are reluctant to divulge over the net.

A typical transaction

Customer confidence should also be increased if a web site can let them know how their e-commerce transaction is being handled. They should then compare this with the number of risks to which they are exposed in a high street or telephone ordering transaction. A card purchase in a high street gives a member of staff access to the card and enters the number in the store's records where other members of staff can see it. It produces two insecure paper copies, one of which can be discarded by the customer, the other of which is in the merchant's system. Add to this the fact that the card could be stolen, or the number taken by the person who is next in the queue and it is a wonder that there is any trust in the system. A telephone transaction is even less secure, but familiarity with it gives people confidence in the system. In many e-commerce systems, the merchant does not even see the credit card number; after all, the merchant has no need to see the number and merely needs to know that the customer has the ability to pay.

Case study

The case study of an e-commerce transaction below demonstrates not only how the system works from the consumer's and the merchant's point of view, but also how the World Wide Web is no respecter of distance. If you want to establish yourself on the other side of the world, then this is reasonably easy. It also demonstrates how, as a business, you can take advantage of the best services offered worldwide as if they were here on your own doorstep.

Alberon.com is a New Zealand-based company which specializes in natural products to promote health and well-being. Its target markets are worldwide, encompassing New Zealand and Australia as a minor market, but also the major population centres of Europe, North America and Asia. Amongst its major lines are health products and supplements, such as shark cartilage and deer velvet (a strength and endurance supplement endorsed by golfer Bob Charles). The business was set up by the consultant for this book and his business partners in 1998 and has continued to trade and grow successfully, relying on organic growth. It is based in New Zealand, one of the most environmentally pure and clean countries left on the earth, and deals in 'look good, feel good' natural products that reflect a clean and green image. This case study looks at what happens when a customer, let's say in Aberdeen, Scotland (about as far away from New Zealand as you can get), logs on to the **Alberon.com** web site and orders several items from it.

The customer (let's call him Angus), deciding that he has a problem with recovery after training, logs onto the web via his own Internet service provider (ISP) through a browser. He logs onto a search engine and, knowing what he wants, enters the term 'deer velvet'. **Alberon.com** has placed this term with several search engines and Angus is directed towards their web site. The web site needs to look good, load quickly, be easy to navigate and contain what Angus is looking for, otherwise he quickly becomes a customer lost. Angus can now browse through the various products and product descriptions at his leisure. He doesn't even need to stay connected to the Internet, but can view the site offline for as long as he needs to make up his mind. Once he has decided on the products that he wants to buy, he can log on again.

He chooses the products which he wants to buy and can have the price displayed in any major currency (the business is going to take payment in $US but why should the customer have the problem of doing the conversion?). At this point, just as with any other shopping trip, Angus puts his purchases in a basket and heads for the virtual version of the supermarket check-out, where he is asked for his credit card details and a full mailing address for delivery purposes (any address as long as it is not a post office box). This is where the virtual transaction starts to become a real one.

The process

Alberon.com lives on a secure server in a super secure building in Chicago, USA. It is hosted by a company called Webfarm which has 170 secure servers in this building. For security purposes, none of the information given by Angus is recorded with Alberon. It is actually recorded on a page hosted by Webfarm to which Alberon has no access (although it is made to look like an integral part of the Alberon site by using their logos, colour scheme etc., as provided by them). This business, in common with virtually every other business on the net, has no need or desire to see a customer's credit card number. In fact, it definitely prefers not to see it. This is one area where web businesses appear to be at a disadvantage when compared to ordinary offline businesses. Customers, perversely, seem quite happy to give their credit card details over a completely insecure telephone line but shy away from placing this information on the net. The fact is that there are no more high-profile cases of fraud on the net than in any other business medium but, because it is a 'new' and exciting, international crime (and because it may have been perpetrated by a 15-year-old in his lonely bedroom), it is given a high profile. This gives the mistaken impression that the web is a less safe place to trade than anywhere else. Web businesses (and **Alberon.com** is no exception) are constantly trying to educate people away from this mistaken point of view. The arrangement with Webfarm means that **Alberon.com** will never have sight of a customer's credit card details – after all, they don't need them.

Angus's intentions have to pass through a secure firewall in order to enter the Chicago part of the operation, where his intention to buy is recorded in US dollars. Let's say that Angus wishes to buy $100 worth of deer velvet and other products. This information needs to be relayed to Alberon, along with information as to how Angus is going to pay and whether he can afford to pay. Chicago now contacts a bank which just happens to be located in Jersey, in the Channel Islands. This bank (The NatWest Bank) runs a system called Worldpay. Worldpay checks Angus's credit card account and, providing he has the funds or the rating, approves the transaction. It then sends out two pieces of information. Firstly, it tells **Alberon.com** that it has an order for $100 worth of products, including deer velvet, and gives them the address to send the products to. It does not pass on any credit card details – it doesn't need to. All Alberon needs to know is that the transaction has been authorized. Worldpay will transfer the money from Angus's account to a holding account for Alberon and, at regular intervals, transfers the balance to Alberon's 'home' bank account in New Zealand.

Secondly, it sends a communication to Angus to let him know that his transaction has been authorized and that the products are on their way. That's all Angus needs to know. He can now happily log off, knowing that he has ordered the products that he wants, his credit card number has been authorized and the products are on their way. What he probably doesn't know is that his credit card number has been protected behind a number of hefty firewalls, the one for the Jersey operation possibly being even more secure than the Chicago one!

Figure 9 shows the way this secure transaction works. From the point of view of Alberon.com, the transaction has had most of the risk taken out of it. If the business took credit card numbers for purchases directly not only would there be security risks, but also the business would have no guarantee that it was dealing with the owner of the card, or that they had the necessary credit. The whole system is actually much more secure and much more certain than an offline transaction – so why do consumers distrust the web so much?

How else can customers pay?

Alberon.com is an example of a site using a trusted third party for their payment system – in this case a bank. The second method is the use of digital cash. A card or similar is loaded with money and this can lead to a direct exchange without sensitive information being passed. One product developed by Sony is called EDY. This has been trialled successfully in Japan. It is a card that can be 'loaded' with money at a cash point or even the local corner shop and electronically read over the net. There is no keying in of details for the customer, and a guarantee of instant payment for the business. This is also considered to be reasonably safe by

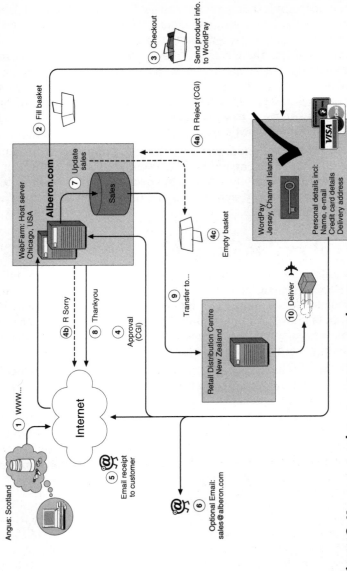

Figure 9 Key events when a customer purchases from alberon.com

consumers, although fraud is still, of course, possible. The difference here is that the fraudster steals money (or value) directly, rather than, as with credit card fraud, the means to steal value. This method is of particular interest to those people trying to access the teenage market. There is £3 billion worth of spending power in this market that e-commerce businesses can't currently access – this is the amount it is estimated that 12-16 year olds would spend on Internet purchases if they were allowed credit cards. Businesses are busy devising ways in which they can tap into this amount such as 'pay-as-you-go' type cards that can be 'loaded' with cash.

The third method, and currently the most popular, is for a credit card number to be entered and then sent in encrypted form. It is in the interests of many businesses to encourage this system as people are familiar and confident with it and its widespread use in the real world of commerce.

Legal problems

Obviously, whilst one of the big advantages of setting up online is the access to the global market place, one of the drawbacks is that you then become subject to the laws of the countries in which you sell. In the UK it is important that your customers are aware of their rights which, put simply, are almost the same as if they had bought a product from a high street shop. So the following apply:

- You have the right to your money back if the product is not delivered (and this must be within a reasonable time).
- Goods should be both 'as described' and 'fit for the purpose' for which they are bought; the Sale of Goods Act and the Supply of Goods and Services Act are the relevant laws which define this condition as being 'of satisfactory quality'.

Further regulations have been framed to govern e-commerce transactions. These are the Department of Trade and Industry Consumer Protection (Distance Selling) Regulations 2000, which were drawn up to help regulate all forms of distance selling. According to these regulations you 'must be given clear information about the goods or services offered', 'after a purchase the consumer must be sent confirmation' and there is now a one-week 'cooling off' period in which you can decide not to go ahead with the purchase. A copy of the new regulations can be found at **dti.gov.uk/cacp/ca/policy/distanceselling/newregs.htm**

Limited liability and floating

The biggest problem for a consumer can occur if the e-commerce company, with limited liability status, goes bust. This is an aspect of trading (not just web trading) that consumers do not always understand. Should the company unfortunately fail, then a liquidator (usually an accountant) will be brought in to handle the sale of the company's assets. If you are a pure dot.com company this may not be much, but will include all your hardware and software (sometimes also even the domain name or brand identity that you have created). This is of no great comfort to a consumer, who may find that they do not receive goods or services ordered but have no way of recovering their payment. However, the failure rate of such companies on the Internet is no worse than that in the high street, so the consumer is actually taking no more risk than usual.

For an Internet trader there are advantages in having limited liability status. By forming a limited company you limit your liability (your responsibility for debt) to just the amount of money you have invested in the company. The act of forming a company gives it a separate legal identity from yourself meaning, in the event of failure, that your personal assets are not at risk. It is a more complex operation to set up a limited company and accounts have to be published, but the advantages usually outweigh the disadvantages – to the extent that there are over a million private limited companies in the UK.

As a private limited company, shares will be held by yourself and just a few other people, they are not on sale to the public. A public limited company goes a step further by selling shares on the stock exchange to raise capital.

Such company launches are how the first round of dot.com companies raised money for further advertising and expansion – of course, this means that their liability has been spread around a large number of shareholders. If and when the company fails, the value of their shares will fall and they may even become worthless. The benefits of success, however, are such that people are willing to take the risk, especially in a sector with so much promise of growth.

You should be careful that the dot.com part of your company, if it fails, does not drag down the 'real' part of your business. If your e-commerce strategy takes place under your current company name, then the assets of your 'real' operation can be used to pay the debts of the 'virtual' one.

Protecting intellectual property

As well as making sure that they can collect the cash, e-commerce operations need to make sure that they respect the integrity of other sites and protect the originality of their own. This means protecting what is yours – your intellectual property – on a worldwide basis. This means that such protection can be subject to different laws operating in different countries. Your site can be accessed from anywhere in the world regardless of where you are actually situated, but is always subject to at least two sets of laws, those in the country where it is based and those in the countries where it is received. One of the trickiest areas is that of intellectual property rights. Physical products can be protected with patents and trade marks that are enforceable in most countries of the world (with a few notable exceptions who earn hard currency by producing forgeries). Copyright laws can be used to protect the written word and, again, they are effective in most countries. The difficulty, as the World Intellectual Property Organization conference in the 1990s pointed out, is that the advent of the Internet has actually made violations of intellectual property a lot easier. The technology, for example, for copying a picture from one site to another, or for taking a chunk of text or even the design template for a web page, has made such theft easier. There are two issues here: how do you protect your own intellectual property on your own web site and what can you do if you feel your intellectual property rights have been broken?

Protecting yourself

To protect your content you can claim copyright and, for anything particularly original or outstanding, apply for a patent. Trade marks can be claimed on logos and even certain phrases which you may wish to associate with your business. Look at Coca-Cola for example. Both Coca-Cola and Coke are trade marks (and, of course, aggressively protected,) but so is the phrase 'the real thing'. This prevents any rival firm from using this famous Coca-Cola advertising tag for their own soft drinks. The only thing that it is not possible to patent is an idea. You can also protect your material by ensuring that, if it is copied, you can prove that the original work is your own. Perhaps you have developmental versions that will do this, perhaps you have a reliable witness who can state that it is your work; better still you can hide markers in your web pages so that you can prove that it is your own work.

With copyright you have to do no more than claim the copyright (put a lower case 'c' in brackets and your PC will produce the copyright symbol for you ©). You don't even need to do this – copyright is automatically yours – but it is usual, in order to make it absolutely clear. As the original author of a piece of text, the copyright is normally yours; this also applies to original design (such as the template for a web page). If you outsource the design of your web site, you will not own the copyright, your outsourcer will. However, you will still hold intellectual rights on things such as your brand names and logos. You can give permission for someone else to use the text or design and, in such cases, it is usual to ask them to state their source or make it clear that you still hold the copyright. This also applies in the other direction – if you want to copy anything from a web site then get in touch with the owner and ask their permission. Generally, if you are not in direct competition with them and agree to credit them as the source, people are quite happy to share. After all, imitation is the sincerest form of flattery. The cases where it may not be are where you are producing text for someone else, in which case they may hold the copyright. One of the lesser known areas of copyright law concerns work that is created whilst you are at work. If you are employed by someone and use their equipment and time to create something then they can claim the copyright. A teacher, for example, using a school computer to write a newspaper article could find that the school owns the copyright and not them. Many employees have created web content or started their web business whilst still an employee and could fall foul of this law.

Registering

To be protected otherwise means that you have to register with the patent office (**www.findit.gov.uk**) or register your trade mark. The warning of 'patent pending' can be used while the registration is processed and, should the patent be allowed, you will be given a number. The ™ symbol is used to denote a trade mark as in 'My product name™'. Registering a patent is, however, not an easy process and should be approached with caution. What it does do, however, is to make enforcement of intellectual property rights much easier. With copyright breaches you will need to prove that someone else has copied your original work; with patent law you have already proven that it is your work through the registration process. Some businesses rely heavily on patents and innovation for their success. Look at Dyson, for example at **www.Dyson.com**.

There is still the problem of those countries that are not parties to the Berne Convention. This is an international treaty which governs intellectual property rights, and in a non-participating country such as Bahrain – where video shops openly sell copies of the latest movies, before they have been released on video – you are going to have little chance of claiming intellectual property rights.

Web links

A copy of the new regulations governing selling over the Internet can be found at **dti.gov.uk/cacp/ca/policy/distanceselling/newregs.htm**.
To protect an invention or similar you need to register with the patent office at **www.findit.gov.uk**.

Business advice on issues such as these in the USA can be found at **www.business.gov**.

!

Hints and tips!

Basic security protection can be provided by using user identities and passwords. Most people's passwords are easy to guess – a household pet, a favourite character from a book or film, a nickname, a date of birth. If you use a password system that requires regular changing of passwords, then this is more secure.

?

Did you know?

Firewalls are installed to be a barrier between a network and the rest of the web. These can check out the web addresses of the people entering a site and even create reports to show who is using the site. They can be used between your PC or network and the rest of the web.

Glossary

Business

limited liability   responsibility for debt is limited to the amount initially invested

floating a company   offering shares for sale to the public

Information Technology

Firewalls   a barrier between two parts of the web which requires security clearance to pass through and which protects against unauthorized access

SMS   Short Messaging Service, often referred to as text messaging

Summary

- The three main problems confronting e-commerce are speed, availability and security.
- There are new solutions to all three problems.
- Credit cards are likely to be replaced by smart cards as a safer way to pay.
- Smart cards will also guarantee the transaction for the merchant.
- Lack of consumer confidence in e-commerce security is misplaced.
- A typical transaction on the web is much more secure than a physical transaction.
- Traders are subject to the laws of the countries in which they are based and those in which they trade.
- Consumers have the same rights buying over the web as they would if they bought from a shop.
- Traders can protect themselves through becoming a limited company.
- They can and should also protect their intellectual property rights.

14 | FORGING STRATEGIC PARTNERSHIPS

'... so long as we both shall make a profit ...'

Partnership strands

This chapter examines three strands of strategic partnerships. Firstly, what sort of partnerships are likely to be necessary to the successful operation of your business; secondly, what sort of extra partnerships you are likely to need as a result of entering the e-commerce arena and thirdly, how you can use the Internet to help you to forge strategic partnerships.

No business operation can survive in complete isolation. This is even more true for Internet-based businesses than it is for those on the high street. It goes without saying that agreements are needed with some essential partners – these partnerships are the necessary building blocks of commercial success. The most important partnership is, of course, between seller and customer, between your successful business and your satisfied customer. In business terms this is a definition of quality. Quality is simply defined as supplying what the customer wants. A quality product is one that fulfils the customer's exact requirements at a price that he or she thinks is fair and gives value for money. Other partnerships may be equally necessary to a successful business operation. Businesses need certainty and continuity of supply, they need support services, and they need assistance and advice. Thus there are important roles to be played by institutions such as banks and other providers of risk capital, by professional service providers such as accountants and lawyers and by trading partners such as suppliers of raw materials or services. The main difference in the e-commerce world compared with the 'real' world is that here some of these partners do not come with the experience and credibility of their 'real' world counterparts. A bank, for example, may have been lending to businesses for a hundred years or more but, because of the newness of the medium, you may be the first e-commerce business that a particular branch operation has been faced with. You are therefore both learning together, and the bank may be much more inclined to lend to an established and traditional business proposition than it is to lend to what it may see as too new and untried.

Bricks and mortar

E-commerce businesses are likely to be coming from one of three directions. They may be large, successful businesses established in the 'real' business world. They are likely to be successful at what they do and are probably regarded as 'major players' in their particular field. They will have money, expertise and resources behind them and enough cash or clout to be able to buy any expertise or advice that they may need. Examples of this type of business could include Virgin and WH Smith. They will be trading, as usual, in the 'bricks and mortar' world of the high street, selling music, books, travel etc., but will have built up a substantial web presence. They will have planned and developed very good, professional web sites (although many web aficionados might condemn them as boring or unimaginative, they have the big advantage that they actually work – and work well). They will be using the Internet and e-commerce as an addition to their current activities, regarding the medium as just another way of reaching a market segment – a different marketing route.

Alternatively they will be much smaller existing businesses, run from the home or from small trading bases, probably providing specialist goods or services. Again, these will usually be successful businesses in their own right which have decided to adapt and extend by building an Internet marketing presence. Fox Saddlers, mentioned in Chapter 2, is one such business. It successfully targets a market for horse and rider related products, which include saddles, bridles and other practical products. Its web site has allowed it to enter new markets all around the world – effectively wherever horse riding is important. Countries with a tradition of horse riding excellence such as Spain, Germany, South America and many of the states of the Arab world have become part of Fox Saddlers market at **www.foxsaddlers.co.uk**. This web site demonstrates a successful expansion of a solid 'real' business into e-commerce trading.

Thirdly, e-commerce businesses may be pure Internet start-ups – these are likely to be businesses with little in the way of an established market base or trading pattern, attempting to hit a potential online market. The key to the success of this sort of business is three-fold. The business needs an original idea (and one that is going to capture the imagination of its intended market), it needs a well-defined and carefully targeted market, and it needs to be able to present its idea clearly and successfully to this target market, convincing them of their need for the product before the business runs out of money.

What support is needed?

In each case as outlined above, the business will need, in order to survive the vicissitudes of the net and of the business world, to have a number of strategic partnerships. For most business operations these will include partnerships with distributors, packagers, wholesalers and suppliers as well as with banks and other risk capital suppliers who back and fund the business. Web-based operations extend this family to include Internet Service Providers, credit card companies and telecommunications organizations.

A traditional business supply chain starts with raw material extraction, then processing and manufacturing, wholesaling and distribution and finally retailing. It involves insurance companies, transport providers, communications organizations and other commercial service providers. One of the aims of many of the 'pure' start-ups was to cut out all or some of these organizations. Little did they realize that not only do you cut your costs, you also cut your levels of knowledge and expertise – transport and distribution providers may be where an organization gets its necessary logistical information and experience from, insurance companies are better placed to estimate levels of risk, communications organizations may be able to advise you on many of the technical aspects of a business that is reliant on good communication for its success. Many purely web-based operations have thus been built on a fairly unstable base, with shallow levels of experience and expertise. This makes them fragile and very vulnerable to change in the market. This fragility and lack of depth is one of the reasons for the downfall of many such businesses. Strategic partnerships with other organizations can limit this vulnerability by strengthening the e-commerce organization.

Quickly come and just as quickly gone!

In terms of growth and survival, the three groups have all fared very differently. The first, big high street names, have been able to support and cosset their online operations to develop web sites where the actual purchase of goods is almost an afterthought. (These web sites may also have the added bonus of being interesting and attractive, but this is not always the case; sometimes they have taken their cue from the staid high street side of the business and produced staid and turgid web sites.) For an example of a good, clear site go and look at the Hodder and Stoughton site (the publishers of this book) at **www.madaboutbooks.com**. You can then compare the difference in approach between this (where actual sales really appear to be something of an afterthought) and a 'pure' Internet operation such as **Amazon.co.uk** which is driven by the need to sell in as much bulk as possible.

The second type of e-commerce organization, the small business operations that have developed an Internet capability, may have been burned by earlier flawed technology if they entered into e-commerce early enough but, on the whole, have fared reasonably well. They have reaped the benefits of their existing partnerships – partnerships that were in the real world – usually involving a niche market selling a real product to a carefully targeted customer but through a fairly traditional and well-supported supply chain. They have had the revenues of a successful business, and the advice and expertise of their successful business partners, to create a good, solid launch pad for an e-commerce venture.

It is the third type of business, the pure Internet business start-ups, that have achieved the most publicity by becoming very big very quickly and then, just as quickly, failing in large and spectacular numbers. They seem to have blossomed and grown at a tremendous rate and then, just as quickly, dried and died. Many (even the supposedly successful operations) failed to ever turn a profit and confidence in the entire sector plummeted as high-profile business after dot.com business collapsed under the weight of its overvaluation and lack of performance.

Many of these businesses have vanished with little trace of their passing – their failure to follow basic business tenets (as outlined in earlier chapters) being the predominant cause of their downfall. They expected to be able to be their own supplier, distributor and sales base, ignoring the traditional partnerships which businesses make with such specialist organizations. If this were possible it should, of course, guarantee healthy profits as the costs of the 'middle man' are cut out. However, there must now be some doubt as to whether a course of action of this nature is ever likely to be a viable business alternative to the traditional approach. And it has succeeded in making life difficult for many of the later arrivals – by creating an area of uncertainty around any pure Internet start-up (even though the technology is now so much better and more efficient) (see Figure 1 on page 2).

Back to basics

Those which have survived the meltdown are beginning to turn back to business basics and are starting to look for established ways into a target market through 'real' world business. Where the first move of a bricks and mortar business may have been to put its catalogue online, many dot.coms now see the need to go the other way and expand into catalogue and other forms of retailing in order to attract customers, eventually, to their web-based operations.

Market research company BMRB reported in its quarterly *Internet Monitor* report (April 2001) that, in six months of the first year of the new millennium – at just the time that Internet start-ups were predicting unlimited growth and astronomical profits – the average amount spent by an Internet purchaser in the UK fell by almost £80 from just over £400 to £326. This does not mean, of course, that there isn't still the potential for phenomenal growth as new businesses and new customers come online: it does mean however, that it is going to be a good idea to follow in the footsteps of successful businesses and develop operations that work together and feed off each other. Trying to sell purely over the Internet means that the business is using only one, very narrow, strategy to attract sales revenue. Successful businesses know that targets should not be focused on a single strategy, but on a combination of strategies that will ensure a width of coverage and a far more stable market and more viable business operation.

Many existing businesses have developed successful strategies for survival which include forging partnerships with other organizations. There is no reason why an e-commerce business should not follow suit. It is important that the businesses that you do commit to partnerships with are strong and well established – joining with a weak partner is just as likely to drag you both down as it is to ensure that you both survive. Remember, a drowning man does not call to another drowning man for help!

'I'll help as much as I can, but I can't swim either...!'

Survivors of the fall

Dot.com survivors have, for example, taken a number of routes back to the biggest traditional market of all – the high street. While the potential of the Internet market may appear unlimited (in theory you can reach every member of the world's population who has access to a computer) it has yet to fulfil that potential, while high street shopping continues to increase. All have involved them in developing strategies that run alongside and support their online operations. Examples of such successful trading include many which require partners such as publishers and distributors, for example:

- establishing a mail order side to the business by publishing and distributing a catalogue
- establishing a mail order side to the business by making arrangements with an existing mail order retailer
- establishing a telesales side to the business
- making a partnership with an existing telesales operation
- working with an established wholesaler and/or distributor

- opening up their own high street retail premises
- supplying a high street retailer with products to sell in their outlets
- supplying an established catalogue retailer with their products
- buying an established high street operation (look at **madaboutwine.com** who now have a number of direct mail wine businesses running alongside their web operation, making strategic use of existing customers, stock and distribution systems)
- buying an existing successful brand name (or even re-launching an unsuccessful one; Clickmango failed as an Internet start-up but is in the process of being successfully re-launched, building on the high levels of customer recognition for the brand).

You might think that, as a small business just starting up in the e-commerce jungle, none of these are opportunities that will be available to you. But think again! Maybe they are not available or appropriate on the same scale, but each can be scaled down to be of some use to even the smallest business.

Real meets virtual

Amazon.com, the struggling but huge Internet retailer, had lost over 80 per cent of its share value in 2000/2001, but in March 2001 recovered strongly on news that a strategic partnership with Wal-Mart, the giant international retailer, could be on the cards. This could signal a major partnership between a real business and an Internet-based one – termed a 'clicks and bricks' partnership. The two could provide many mutual benefits, feeding off each other's operations. Amazon could be employed – with its field of expertise – to handle and develop Wal-Mart's online strategy and sales while Wal-Mart could provide a real and well-established market for Amazon's services. Wal-Mart is the largest retailer in the world but has failed to make any real headway with its Internet business **www.walmart.com**, whereas Amazon is the acknowledged leader in its Internet field but is struggling to make any profit from its operations. A partnership such as the proposed one could be of tremendous benefit to both companies.

Such a partnership is an example of what is becoming known as 'affiliate marketing'. Instead of an e-commerce business trying to attract advertisers in order to generate revenue, they partner up with other businesses and provide links to each other's sites and to each other's on- or off-screen enterprises. Interested in vegetarian or vegan products? Then a link from a vegetarian information site to (for example) the Linda McCartney range of vegetarian foods could be followed by a link from this site to a retailer of such foods. This system is already well established in the United States where it is often possible to 'click through' to another site just by clicking on the business's logo or some other form of hyper-link. A commission on sales generated in this way is the reward for the affiliate site; an increased customer base and increased sales is the reward for the e-commerce business. Businesses have also discovered that once the customer has found a specific site, they will return straight to that site if they want more purchases, rather than going through the affiliate. In many cases therefore, the business only incurs a commission charge to the affiliate on the first-time buyer – it then 'captures' the customer for itself. Amazon has over ten thousand affiliate sites pointing users in its direction and other large sites will soon be able to match this. A partnership with Wal-Mart could see Wal-Mart users 'clicking through' to Amazon, and Amazon users 'clicking through' to Wal-Mart. Online intermediaries such as Amazon (who, after all, don't actually publish books) rely almost entirely on publishers and distributors to ensure that they have the necessary stock and that it can be delivered to customers. Without strategic partnerships, such businesses could not exist

For your own business, you should look for likely partners that will be able to push traffic your way. Perhaps you sell something that has a number of complements? Then you have the opportunity of partnering up with a business that sells them. There are even suppliers on the web who will register partners and track transactions for you, letting you know which of your affiliates is generating what trade (try **www.befree.com** based in the United States or **www.ukaffiliates.com** in the UK).

Using existing partnerships

As an existing successful business with the intention of expanding into e-commerce you will already have many of the solid partnerships with suppliers, distributors, suppliers of risk capital and so forth and should not be looking for new partners. You should, initially, see what help and expertise they can offer. After all, you already trust and work with them, why go to other people? You will find that most have recognized the need to provide help and advice in this new market place and so have developed levels of expertise in the new areas. Quite often this expertise will be available at no or low cost. Banks, for example, may be more concerned in getting and keeping your business than in charging you for advice of this nature – especially as the advice is likely to make their own investment in you a lower risk.

Different partners

For an e-commerce operation you will not just need conventional partners, however, but a whole new tranche of technical partners such as web designers and hosts, ISPs and telecommunications providers. Again, some of your existing partners may have developed technical expertise in order to provide advice on these services, so it is worth going to them to see what is on offer before going to anyone else – the first place to call should be your bank.

Some banks are much more 'switched on' to the opportunities than others. See what your normal bank can do for you first and then look around at what deals are offered by other banks. Some charge a fee whereas others don't, and the fees that are charged may vary considerably from bank to bank. Some will be more keen to finance e-commerce ventures than others and may, for instance, provide better online payment systems. You don't have to stick with your existing bank – changing bank accounts is reasonably painless these days.

Partnerships with other businesses

One simple and effective way of gaining the benefits of partnering is to join with another business with similar requirements to yours.

This needs to be a similar organization – i.e. if you are a small and personalized organization, you need a partner who shares a similar structure and goals. Such partners do not have to be competitors. In fact, it would be foolish to partner with a competitor business if this meant sharing your own hard-won contacts with it. But there is little reason why a small business should not partner another small business. For example, a small business selling electrical goods could benefit from a partnership with a small business selling stationery. An electrical goods retailer will have a need for stationery and a stationers will need certain electrical goods, but this is of small importance compared to the other benefits. The businesses will have similar technical requirements and could share software, hardware and expertise. While they would be unlikely to share a web site, they could share payment and distribution systems at a reduced cost to both businesses. It could be even more advantageous if the two businesses were in the same line of business but were occupying different slots in the same chain of distribution. For example, the electrical retailer could go into a partnership with an electrical wholesaler or with a business dealing in electrical repairs. Each then grows with the help of the others by sharing not just technical expertise and logistics but also customer contacts.

In hosting links to other businesses' web sites the key is to try to choose connections but not competitors. You don't want your customers to find you (thanks to your excellent marketing and or reputation) and then immediately click on a link to your nearest competitor. You do want those who visit related sites, however, to click through to yours. So you have to think carefully about whose web links you are going to be willing to host on your site and which sites you want to be on reciprocally. For example, as a seller of consultancy services specializing in the educational market you would not wish to be linked with a site offering similar educational services. You could, however, be linked with other consultancy sites, specializing in other areas. Better still would be to find a site that complemented yours in some way. Perhaps a provider of online lessons or a supplier of school equipment would be useful. Best of all would be to find a site that did offer educational consultancy, but not services that were in direct competition with your own. A truly complementary site would offer goods or services that fitted well with your products but were not in direct competition with them.

Web rings

Another way of working with partner sites is to join a web ring. These are sites of similar interest linked to each other by hyper-links. A visitor can jump from one site directly to the other. You may find that the best sort of web ring to join actually contains sites which are competing for your business but you should not allow this to put you off. At least once a visitor is within the ring, you have a potential customer who is interested in buying from one of the businesses. So you have the chance of a customer looking for a specific product arriving at your site via a web ring rather than a search engine. You also have the further advantage that, if a competitor is not quite able to fulfil a particular customer's needs, they are just a click away from your own site. It is a little like the areas which have always grown up in great trading cities – the goldsmiths' area, the shoemakers' area and so on. Potential customers knew where to go and could browse round a number of outlets until finding one that had what they wanted. The outlet that was not in with the others actually suffered a disadvantage from its isolation – the group was easier to find and promised more choice than the individual shop so was always going to attract more customers.

Partnerships with virtual communities

Virtual communities are groups of people who join together online to share a common hobby or purpose. A partnership with such a community can be a powerful marketing tool. The idea of **www.letsbuyit.com** was to create a virtual community of like-minded people – consumers who wanted to obtain goods or services at advantageously low prices – and to use this to put pressure on manufacturers and suppliers to lower prices. Buying in bulk should always make the product cheaper than the purchasing of individual items or items in small numbers. How can the small business take advantage of such communities? There are two ways of doing this, one is to endeavour to build such a community yourself. For example, a number of sites selling health or health-related products (from exercise bikes to dietary supplements) could assist in the creation of a virtual community keen to buy such products. Alternatively, a small business could seek out an existing community of this nature and offer better value and better service than its larger competitors. By finding such a community (which it may be possible to do through newsgroups) it has already identified its target niche market and therefore has saved itself a lot of work in advertising and promotion.

Passing the word along

You will also need good partnerships with those businesses that you rely on to provide the other parts of your chain of distribution. Your suppliers need to be reliable and aware of your likely new requirements, your technical partners need to be reliable and trustworthy and, of course, you must not forget your customers. Your biggest and most important partnership is with your customer, – whether existing or potential.

You will know from your non-Internet marketing and existing business that the best way to gain new customers (whilst ensuring that you retain the old ones) is through personal recommendation or word of mouth. A satisfied customer or a pleased supplier is a better, cheaper and more effective advertisement than any that you will ever pay for. Why blow your own trumpet, and pay for the privilege, when you can get someone else to do it for you for free and a great deal more effectively. So keep your customers and other partners sweet and they will quickly let the rest of the world know that you are the best. You can use this to your advantage by collecting feedback from customers and using it in your marketing. Customers who say that they have had a good deal from you, or have found that the service was excellent, or make any comments which relate, in particular, to the value that you have added to their purchasing experience, can be used both on the web site and off it. If there are demonstrations of customer loyalty or satisfaction that you can put up on the site (a photograph of a successfully completed product for a designer, for example) then these can also be powerful tools.

Web links

An example of a site that has grown out of a successful business is **www.madaboutbooks.com** while **www.amazon.co.uk** is a 'pure' Internet site. Affiliate marketing sites can be found at **www.befree.com** based in the United States or **www.ukaffiliates.com** based in the UK.

! Hints and tips!

Don't just look for partners in your own country – it is just as easy to partner up with someone from across the world. It may be that the best partner for you is one who provides the same product but, for example through a different language. Most web content is conducted through English but this could mean that you are missing enormous market potential. Think of the size of the Chinese market, for example, as China joins the global market place.

? Did you know?

Partnerships between respectable 'real' world businesses and certain other markets have made inroads into certain markets. The pornography industry is no longer confined to dark and dingy back alleys, nor the preserve of suspicious looking types in long grey macs. Pornography is a £5 blllion industry worldwide. It is so lucrative that many big companies have decided to join in quietly. Who do you think, for example, pipes the blue movie pay per view channels into many of the top hotels around the world? The American AT&T telecommunications company owns the Hot Network sex channel; General Motors holds a company called DirectTV, which carries out a similar function.

Glossary

Business

strategic partnerships   important and necessary links both within and outside businesses

bricks and mortar businesses   established in the 'real' rather than the 'virtual' world of trading

affiliate marketing   forming partnerships with sites (affiliates) that provide links to your site

clicks and bricks   a partnership between a 'virtual world' business and a 'real world' business

Information Technology

click through   going straight to another web site by clicking on a hyper-link

web ring   a series of sites sharing a common product or purpose all joined together by hyper-links

virtual communities   groups of web users who have joined together to share a common purpose

Summary

- Partnerships are just as important in e-commerce operations as in 'real' business, perhaps more so.
- E-commerce entrants are either big businesses enhancing their real business, small businesses growing on the net or pure e-commerce start-ups.
- Partnerships are vital to each of them and include suppliers, logistics and other ancillary services – businesses need to make use of their expertise.
- Many first-round Internet businesses tried to bypass partnerships, with disastrous results.
- Businesses established or based in one world (real or virtual) can become stronger by finding partners in the other world.
- Affiliates can be found on the web who will push trade your way

- Successful partnerships can be forged with businesses in the same sector as yours.
- There are a number of ways of finding partners using the Internet.
- Your customers are your most important partners, use word-of-mouth recommendation wherever possible.

15 | MANAGING PEOPLE AND PROCESSES

'You may look wonderful now, but you aren't half as efficient as me!'

As an owner, entrepreneur or employer, you are likely to have immediate concern as to how much the move into e-commerce will affect the other strategic parts of your organization. You will be concerned as to how it will affect your organization, your people and your processes. You will want to make sure that the effect on these vital elements of your business is a positive one. You may be a business with many employees, or just a few. Even if you are a sole proprietor with no employees at all, you should still be concerned as to how the change will actually affect you. You should also consider your customers, suppliers and other external agencies with which you have dealings. Sensibly, you will want your new strategy to enhance and improve the relationships with these groups rather than cause any friction.

Of course, in an organization which has a structure and employees, managing change will be a skill which the management will need to have already acquired. This chapter looks at how the skills of change management can be applied to the introduction of an e-commerce element to your business.

Planning for change

You need to make sure that the changes that you are going to make are planned carefully. Many businesses have leapt into the e-commerce revolution with little or no thought as to where their strategy is going to take them – in fact, you might be hard put to say that they have a strategy at all. If your growth path at the moment consists of 'get a web site because we must have one … and then erm...' then you need to think again. Writing a proposed growth path would be a good idea; creating a growth path with intermediate targets would be an even better one. There are three parts to this: you need to be able to see where the business is now, where you would like it to be, and how you intend to get there. Unplanned changes are much more difficult to manage and yet, amazingly, this is how many businesses approach their venture into e-commerce. They first buy a machine, and then they decide that they want a web site. They build it, launch it, admire it and then begin to wonder what the purpose of it is. Strategic planning is essential for a smooth introduction. Treat it like any other part of a business expansion. If you were a retail outlet that was going to open a new branch you would go through a very careful process. This would include looking at the location (and possible alternatives), the design and layout of the shop, where you will draw customers from, where and when suppliers can make deliveries and, perhaps most importantly, a careful and detailed process for the appointment of good staff. Treat e-commerce with as much care as you would any other type of expansion to your existing business.

Control

It is important that you retain control over the way that the changes are introduced into your business. The introduction of e-commerce is, of course, an internal change, so should stay within your control, but it also involves external factors – such as the reaction of your staff or customers to the new technology. However, unlike most internal changes, you will not keep complete control once your e-commerce side goes 'live'. In providing a route for customers or suppliers to reach you, you will also have provided a way for your staff to reach the Internet. It is this influence that needs to be minimized so that it causes the least possible disruption. You need to decide what sort of access, at what level, your staff are going to be entitled to, and manage the introduction of this so that it is seen to be fair and equitable to all. This sort of control can also be applied to yourself if you are a sole proprietor – except in this case, it's self control! There is nothing easier than getting sidetracked from what you ought to be doing than by being beckoned by this whole new world that opens up in front of you. For many, thankfully, the Internet will not be a novelty. They will have access at home or have been introduced to it at work. This may mean, though, that they already have favourite sites or uses to which the Internet can be put. The same applies to you. How easy will you find it to keep your Internet-enabled business purely for business?

People, both within and outside your business, will be full of helpful and not so helpful advice. Some will have tales to tell of how e-commerce has improved their business immeasurably. (It is possible; British Telecom, advertising its web site help for business, quotes a firm called Red Shark, which claims that its business of selling printer cartridges has increased twenty-fold after working with BT products. Of course, it is in their interest to say so.) Others will have horror stories of business failure, of how businesses have been ripped off, or exposed themselves to enormous and uncontrollable costs (and will take great delight in telling them to you). Don't disregard such people, listen to what they have to say, then collect evidence from other, less personally involved sources, and finally make a decision. It is important that it is you who makes the decision. You must stay in control.

Resistance to change

Your people may welcome the change or they may resist it. The reaction could well depend on how the change is introduced. New technology has often been seen as posing a threat to people's jobs (even though, in the long run, most new technology creates jobs). It has always been thus. In the nineteenth century, Ned Lud and his band of machine breakers – the Luddites or Shatterers – feared for their livelihoods when machinery was introduced into textile manufacture (so went round smashing the machines). Trains, motor cars and even bicycles were treated with extreme caution before gaining respectability, and is surely true that telegraph operators trembled in their boots when the telephone was invented. But you can't stop progress.

Resistance is likely to come in one of two directions – the established staff who feel their position is threatened by new technology and new methods, and the young and thrusting who feel that you have not gone far enough. The obvious area of resistance may be the established staff, and they may have already suffered from the inexorable advance of new technology. Examples might include the tracer or graphic designer who sees the CAD machine reducing their skilled job to a level available to anyone, or the filing clerk or secretary who sees his or her role taken over by a database. There may be a case for retraining; there will certainly be a case for explaining the possible gains and ensuring that these staff benefit from them.

The other likely problem can come from those who have some knowledge of the new technology. These may be well trained and knowledgeable – in which case they will prove to be an asset to your business if you can harness their talents – or they may prove to be someone with 'a little knowledge'. Often this person will decide that your strategy has not gone far enough and bombard you with suggestions. There is no harm in listening to these, but you should always be the one that actually makes the decisions. At worst, they may begin to interfere with your systems in order to 'enhance' them to levels at which they think they should be. This must not be allowed to happen.

Other important groups of people who will possibly be affected by the changes you introduce include suppliers and customers. Some will prefer to stick by the old, tried and tested ways of operating, whatever new alternatives you offer. This is why you should never discard the 'old' way of doing things just because you have a new one. The two should be allowed to run alongside each other and, if it is your intention to get rid of the old way and operate only through e-commerce applications, then this should be a gradual, phased transition. The costs to you can be offset against the greater confidence that customers and suppliers will have in your systems once they see that they are effective.

Persuasion

The best managers of people and organizations are those who are able to persuade their people that the change is in their own best interests – that they will gain more from the change than they are likely to lose. Be proactive in this rather than reactive. In other words, anticipate the likely problems and objections and have solutions in place rather than (as often happens) hoping that everything will be all right and then having no strategy to cope with it if it doesn't turn out as you had hoped! If you can persuade your people that the change is in their best interests then they will actively support it and make the process of change so much easier. If the things that people have worked for are seen as coming under threat – their status in the organization, their established routine, their formal or informal groupings, their income – then there will be resistance to change. So long as you can persuade them that those things which they feel are important will be retained, or even enhanced, then people will support rather than resist change.

Your e-commerce strategy doesn't mean that you have to have put dot.com after the name of your business in order to enhance the status of your people, who could then see themselves as working for a 'cutting edge' organization (in fact, some see it as a disadvantage – see Did You Know? page 230). There are other ways that you can enhance the status of your business. One benefit for staff should be a personal e-mail address each at the business. Little things like ordering up some new business cards with the web site and a personal e-mail address on it can help to maintain or increase status. For a small cash outlay you can have staff feeling that they have benefited in some way and are a part of the change, not non-participant observers. This means that, of course, you must be prepared to allow your staff to use the e-mail! Other, equally simple devices can be used for the same purpose – extras that have come about as a direct result of your expansion but which show that you value your staff. Customers and suppliers can also receive benefits. If it is cheaper for you to make or take orders via e-commerce then a part of that saving should be passed on to your stakeholders. Make e-commerce orders discounted orders, make certain special offers available only via your web site, and reward customers for using the web site or for visiting it a certain number of times (over a reasonable period of time).

Remember, part of the advantage to you of being online is the ability to shop around for cheaper suppliers. You may also find that suppliers use similar techniques to the ones mentioned above. Pay attention to these and see what discounts or other advantages you can gain. Then, just as importantly, see which of these strategies can be applied to your own e-commerce operations or web site.

Structure

As well as people, the structure of the organization can make change management difficult. Some organizations are governed by rules, regulations and usual practice. For some types of business change will be harder than others because of the way in which the business is structured or managed. If you are a business which practises law, for example, you will want to have a reputation for stability (even being staid) and will need to present your e-commerce expansion as something that will not dent that reputation. This will be important to clients as well as to your staff. If you are a business which already deals in commodities or services that might be described as 'new economy', then there will be much less resistance to change.

There may still, however, be 'certain ways' in which things are done or 'have always been done' and you will need to recognize the need to change these as is appropriate, and plan such change into your strategy. The more flexible your organization structure and the more adaptable your leadership style, the easier the process will be. If you can see that the structure of the organization might get in the way of the strategy then you have two choices: either change the structure so that it does not conflict with the strategy or change the strategy so that it does not conflict with the structure. You will need to use your knowledge and experience of the business to decide which of these is the most likely to be successful. It will depend on how flexible the strategy is or can be, and on how important the structure, ethos and culture of your business is to its success. Whatever you decide, you must manage the change without losing the overall direction and thrust of the strategy.

Intelligent businesses

Intelligent businesses are those which are able to recognize and judge where they are and then plan change gradually through a process that sees the need for change, maps the change out, wins support for the change and only then executes it. The four elements to a change management programme are technology, systems, skills and organization and culture and values.

- **Technology**. This is the point where the change will be engendered so will be the first part of the organization to look at. See where new technology is necessary and where it is desirable. See where it is not necessary and, most importantly, where it is not desirable. For example, a new technology element to a traditional law firm at the point where clients interface with staff is likely to lose more custom than it will gain. E-commerce is not always a necessary adjunct to all parts of a business; in this case, it is likely that the client-to-customer interface will be much more effective if it is conducted as it always has been – face to face.

- **Systems**. These can be changed by the introduction of new technology. It is up to you, in managing the changes, to make sure that they are of benefit to the business. Think about the various systems that you have in place, for example, for ordering stock, accepting orders and customer service. Which of these needs to be left alone? Which needs to run in parallel with new systems? Which can be discarded? You should make a list of all the systems that you have in place and then see into which category they fall. There may also be a fourth category – this will consist of those systems which you are now able to use but which you weren't able to before – these could be online banking or credit, or the ability to take credit and debit card orders and micro-payments through your web site.

- **Skills and organization**. One of the basic errors often made by people expanding a business (in any direction, let alone into e-commerce) is to undervalue the existing skills which they have in the organization. It is likely to be well worth your while to find out what skills your staff have – you may find that someone is already adept at web site design, or may even have their own web site (many people now have a personal web site as a way of keeping in touch with friends and family around the world, for example). At the very least you will identify the staff that are willing and able to be trained. There is no point buying skills in if you already have them but are currently under-using them.

- **The organization**. This may be of a type that resists change. Some organizations may be hidebound by rules, frameworks and traditions. It is your job, as an effective manager – whether a sole trader or manager of a large organization – to ensure that the organization is sufficiently flexible. This will depend, at least partly, on the culture within which your business operates.

- **Culture and values**. These are the ways in which the organization operates, and the standards which it expects. They refer to the way in which people within the organization are expected to treat each other and how they are expected to deal with external stakeholders. Your mission and objectives will be strongly linked to the values which you have as a business. As a sole trader, your business is likely to operate on what is called a 'power' culture'. All this means is that you, as the owner, are the dominating force in the business, as you are the main decision-maker. One of the major decisions that you will have to make is whether you will remain in charge of the e-commerce side of your business or will be willing to delegate power to someone else. People operating in power cultures tend to find it difficult to achieve this!

In larger organizations you may have less control over the organization's culture, but you will always need to take the culture into account before going forward with your strategy. Some cultures will give fewer problems than others. For example, a dynamic culture such as a task culture – where teams are set up and dissolved according to the best way of completing a specific task – will have a head start on other organizations. One example of this type of culture could be a consultancy business, which will be able to design its e-commerce strategy so that it takes advantage of the dynamic structure that already exists. If you feel that you are operating in a different and more difficult culture, you may have to set about changing it if your e-commerce strategy is to succeed.

People

As outlined on page 224, you need to find out what levels of expertise already exist amongst your people. What knowledge and skills do you need? What can you best make use of? How easy is it to enhance these levels? Consider your training needs: do you personally need training (a good idea if you are going to be able to oversee your e-commerce operation – you don't want to be left in the dark by your staff)? Do your staff need training? If so, which ones and to what level? Where can you get the training? Some training courses are free – the UK government runs an Internet skills training course (with basic certification). Sometimes forms of training will come as part of the package with new equipment that you have bought; sometimes it can take place online. Many manufacturer and supplier sites run an FAQ (Frequently Asked Questions) section that can save you paying for expensive advice elsewhere. Newsgroups and other forums can also be used before setting out on the purchase of commercial training packages.

Having said that, however, as far as computers are concerned, the best sort of training is having someone sit by you and guide you through the various processes and pitfalls. All the better if you have someone on your staff who can achieve this.

Stakeholders

Stakeholders are any person or body that has an interest in the success of your business. You, of course, are a major stakeholder in your own business, but so are your customers, your suppliers, your employees, your bank (and any other creditors). These are all people who will need to be kept informed of your e-commerce strategy and who you may wish to bring on board at various stages. Your creditors may need to be approached with a business plan outlining your aims and kept informed at each stage of your progress – they will want your e-commerce venture to be as risk free as possible. Suppliers will also be interested in the benefits that they might gain and in what new ways they may be expected to operate.

Finally, your customers will need to be persuaded of the benefits of using the new strategies that you have put into place.

Processes

The processes within your business are the ways in which various tasks are carried out. These may be manufacturing or production tasks (producing a service, for example) or could just be the process by which you carry out sales, deliveries, finance or customer service. You will need to identify the key processes in your business and then decide which of these will benefit from e-commerce. As mentioned before, it is imperative that the 'old' processes are not discarded, but that they are run in tandem with the new ones. There are two reasons for this. Firstly, your new processes may either not work or be subject to unforeseen problems; obviously, in the meantime you need your old processes to stay in place. Secondly, some of your stakeholders may not wish to use or be willing to adapt to new processes or methodologies. Even if you see them as being much more efficient this may not be the case for others. Remember, you will have gone through your period of e-commerce change, they may only just be starting theirs. This is one of the reasons why it is so important to keep stakeholders informed of both your plans and your progress.

Size and change

Many businesses contemplating a move into e-commerce will be SMEs – small- to medium-sized enterprises. Many will be micro-businesses and have fewer than ten employees. Many are bound to be sole proprietors, where the decision-making and change management all has to be handled by a single person, along with all of their other responsibilities. This is one reason why many small businesses either don't venture into e-commerce or only venture into it in a minimalist way – i.e. an e-mail address or a very simple web site.

Sole proprietors should remember, however, that they do not have to take all of their decisions without any help – and that there is help out there which they can get for free. The professional advice from lawyers, accountants and independent financial advisers will be costly, but there are other areas to be tapped into. These include government help (at both local and national level), local trade organizations and business networking. Even some commercial help is free – banks, for example, may run an advice service. National government has a web site (see pages 7, 57), where help and advice can be gained; local councils will also provide advice and assistance. Organizations such as local Chambers of Trade and Chambers of Commerce exist to help small businesses to make decisions, but perhaps the most powerful (and free) tool is business networking. This means that you just talk to your fellow business people on an informal basis to try to glean what good points they have discovered and what mistakes they have made. You can then make sure that you don't make the same errors!

Larger businesses will be able to call on the services of experts in various fields. Managers or owners of larger businesses should first try to find out if they already have the necessary e-commerce talent in-house – remember as said above, there is no point buying skills in if you already have them but are under-using them. In a large business it will be important to delegate someone as being responsible for your e-commerce strategy and to give them the power to carry it forward. You will need to retain a good balance between the freedom which you give them (and they must have some freedom to be adventurous, creative or innovative) and the control which you exercise over them. This is the key to good delegation.

Managing growth

Once you feel that your expansion into web-based business is secure, you can begin to look at the effects of this on the rest of your business. You may find that you need to restructure your business to take account of the e-commerce element. Perhaps you are now taking more orders – you will (hopefully) be taking more remote orders than before and these will need shipping. Don't just develop the e-commerce side but, using your business plan as a guide (see Chapter 5), rebuild your operation from the bottom upwards. E-commerce will show up any problems that your organization already has – and is likely to make them even bigger. If, for example, your business is inefficient at sending out orders, an e-commerce arm is not going to improve this, it is actually going to make it worse. How so? Well, if your e-commerce strategy is successful, you will multiply your orders, and this means that your inefficiency will therefore also multiply. If you can't get a certain volume of orders out quickly now, then you are unlikely to be able to cope with an increased volume. This underlines the fact that 'real' business issues (and practices) are inextricably tied up with e-commerce ones, and that e-commerce cannot avoid ether the problems or necessary discipline of 'real' business – because it is real business!

Time management

An e-commerce strategy can quickly do one of two (equally undesirable) things if not managed properly. It can either stagnate as you don't have the time to keep it up to date, or it can grow to fill all the important time that you previously had allocated to other projects. In a large business the problem is one of deciding how much time should be given to your expert to run a web site and expand the strategy. This will depend on whether they are someone that you have bought in specifically for the job – in which case they will spend 100 per cent of their time on it (can you afford this, for how long?) – or whether you have given someone time away from their normal duties. In this case, how much time? And who is going to pick up the normal duties that they now no longer have time to perform? As a sole proprietor it is even more imperative that you are disciplined in your approach – otherwise you could very quickly find yourself spending not enough or too much time on your strategy. Lay aside a specific time slot and stick to it!

Conclusion

Don't assume that, because you can manage your business successfully, you can automatically transfer that business to an e-commerce element. It is important to realize that, while many of the challenges and problems of e-commerce are nothing more than the problems of ordinary business with an 'e-' on the front, there are problems and pitfalls that are unique to it. Proceeding with careful planning, listening to any advice that is offered (but not necessarily following it) and keeping all of your people on board are tactics that will increase the likelihood of a successful transition.

! **Hints and tips!**

The key to managing change well is often just keeping people informed. This doesn't mean just the key people in the organization, but everyone who may be affected by it. If you can combine the information with some idea of the benefits that this will bring to your people, all the better. If it is just you, you still need to be aware of the benefits that an e-commerce strategy can bring to you. Make a list of the good points and keep adding to it as you think of more. You'll be surprised!

? **Did you know?**

One business at least has decided to drop the dot.com from its name as it was not seen to be doing the company any good. **Getmapping.com** reverted to plain **Getmapping** (the company deals in aerial photography) so that people would not think of the business as 'just an Internet company'. This was at a time (March 2001) when the stock of dot.com companies was seen to be at a particularly low point. The story was particularly newsworthy as the Queen is a shareholder in the company.

Web links

Two possible sites for training matters are **www.computerskillscentres.com** (The London e-commerce academy) and **www.fastrack-it.com**. There are many, many others. Universities and colleges often have courses on which you can enrol and many local schools also offer twilight courses (try **schoolsnet.com** for a complete list of UK schools and contacts).

Glossary

Business

sole proprietor   a business owned and controlled by a single person; this does not necessarily mean that there are no employees

stakeholders   any person or group of people with an interest in the success of your business

managing change   making sure that the process of change in your organization is as smooth and painless as possible

intelligent businesses   those which are able to recognize and judge where they are and then plan change gradually through a change management programme

power culture   businesses that are dominated by a single powerful individual (often sole traders)

Information Technology

CAD   Computer Aided Design, often linked with **CAM** – Computer Aided Manufacture

Summary

- Business people will be concerned as to how e-commerce will affect their organization, their people and their processes.
- It is important that the e-commerce strategy is a carefully planned one.
- Listen to the advice of others, but sift it carefully before acting on it; above all, don't be put off by horror stories.
- It is a good idea to run old and new systems in tandem.
- Think about the benefits that you can pass on to staff if you want their support.
- Think carefully before putting 'dot.com' in your business's name – it may not always be a good idea.
- The structure, values and culture of the organization may pose the greatest resistance to change.
- Find out and use the skills, knowledge and expertise which you already have in your business.
- Be prepared to train both yourself and your staff if necessary.
- Keep stakeholders 'on board' by keeping them informed of progress.

GLOSSARY

Business

action planning   detailed plans which include how to reach objectives, who is responsible, when things should have happened by and what to do if they haven't

adding value   persuading customers to buy more than they had originally intended; encouraging return custom; also called 'selling up'

affiliate marketing   forming partnerships with sites (affiliates) that provide links to your site

blue sky market   a market with no competition as yet

BRAD   directory of publications with circulation figures and advertisement prices; expensive to buy but generally available in the reference section of your local library

brand   a word/words or symbol, rendered in a specific way, that identifies that this product is made by this business, e.g. Johnnie Walker for a particular Scotch whisky

brand identity   recognition of a business through a name, colour scheme, logo, tag line etc.

brand image   the 'message' which a business manages to give through logos, colour schemes, slogans etc.; linked to the values and aims of the business

break-even   where your revenues equal your costs

bricks and mortar businesses   established in the 'real' rather than the 'virtual' world of trading

burn rate   the rate at which a business burns (or spends) its initial capital; a high burn rate means that the cash is soon spent

cash flow   a prediction of the amount of money flowing into and out of a business

clicks and bricks   a partnership between a 'virtual world' business and a 'real world'

complement   products which are bought at the same time to be used with your product

corporate identity   the way a company or business projects its image, through devices such as company colours, uniforms, use of standard fonts, standard designs etc. – just look round in your local supermarket to see this at work

Deming, W. E. (1900–93)   American engineer hailed as the 'father' of quality management

disintermediation   the process of cutting out the middleman

floating a company   offering shares for sale to the public

gap in the market   a discovered or created 'gap' where demand has not yet been tapped

globalization   or global markets; the increasing trend for businesses to operate with little or no regard for national and international boundaries; businesses can produce where labour is cheap, operate from countries whose laws favour them and declare profits in low tax areas

hacking   illegally entering a computer system

halo effect   the way a good brand can promote sales of other products

intellectual property   the right of a person to assert that 'this is mine' and should not be copied

intelligent businesses   those able to recognize and judge where they are and then plan change gradually through a change management programme

intermediation   acting as the middleman

limited liability   responsibility for debt is limited to the amount initially invested

liquidity ratios   show how capable your business is of paying its debt

logo   the symbol that represents the business; there are some very powerful ones – e.g. the Nike tick, the Unilever 'U', the Johnnie Walker 'man with walking stick'

managing change   making sure that the process of change in your organization is as smooth and painless as possible

margins   a measure of the amount of profit that can be made on a sale

market-led innovation   a gap in the market has a product created or developed to fill it

market research   finding out information about your market or potential market

marketing mix   the mixture of price, promotion, product and distribution used to increase sales

media   the way in which messages are passed from your business to your prospective customers

micro-businesses   a European Union definition of those businesses with fewer than ten employees

netspionage   hacking into a system in order to obtain sensitive or secret commercial information

networks, networking   often some of the most important assets of a business are the people that you talk to, those in other businesses or different fields with whom you can share experience or bounce ideas around; these are your business networks and networking can be an important tool of management

new economy   businesses which are involved in computers and information technology; businesses which have embraced new e-technology

niche market   a small or concentrated part of a market segment

non-price competition   competing through promotions, offers and extras rather than on price

old economy   everybody else in business (particularly used to refer to staid 'old' businesses such as banking and insurance although many have grasped new technology more readily than others)

organic growth   slow but sustainable growth of a business

perfect substitute   a product so near to yours as to be identical; try to avoid competing in this area

PEST analysis   a way of analysing a number of external factors to see which ones are having the most effect on your business and which can be used to your advantage

pester power   advertising term coined to describe the power that children have to persuade parents to buy

power culture businesses that are dominated by a single powerful individual (often sole traders)

product extension strategies changing, developing or upgrading a product so that sales can be maintained

product-led innovation the product is developed first, then the gap in the market is created

product life cycle the natural cycle that a product goes through from its initial launch to its final demise

pull strategy getting the customer to come to you rather than you going to the customer

quality a product that is perfectly fitted to its purpose

re-intermediation acting as your own middleman

remote sales selling that is not face-to-face; telephone, catalogue, mail order and e-commerce sales

risk capital money which investors are willing to risk

ROCE Return On Capital Employed – important in showing whether your business is using the money you have invested in it efficiently

SMART targets a way of defining certain aims; SMART usually stands for targets that are Specific, Measurable, Attainable, Relevant and Time related

SMEs small- and medium-sized enterprises; defined in the UK as businesses with fewer than 250 employees

sole proprietor a business owned and controlled by a single person; this does not necessarily mean that there are no employees

stakeholders any person or group of people with an interest in the success of your business

strategic partnerships important and necessary links both within and outside businesses

strategic planning this involves a business asking itself a number of key questions about where it is and where it wants to be

substitute a product that is in competition

SWOT analysis this is a technique for highlighting the internal strengths and weaknesses of your business and the external opportunities and threats to it

tag line a catchy phrase that identifies your business

teasers short phrases which describe stories inside a publication; meant to persuade you to buy it

test marketing marketing a product in a restricted area first, in order to gauge consumer reaction

TQM (Total Quality Management) a culture where everyone in an organization is responsible for quality, not just a designated few

trade mark a sign or name belonging to a business and protected in law

trialling testing a product on a small number of people, or in a particular situation

USP Unique Selling Point – what makes your product special

venture capital money made available to risk on new enterprises

Information Technology

ADSL Asymmetric Digital Subscriber Line, able to transmit digital information at high bandwidths

ASP Application Service Providers are similar to ISPs except that they tend to concentrate on the business side of the net

B2B business to business

B2C business to consumer (retailing)

B2G business to government

bold fonts that are rendered so that they are dark – **like this**

broadband a faster connection to the Internet

CAD Computer Aided Design, often linked with

CAM Computer Aided Manufacture

CD/RW drives a drive that will both read and write to CDs

chatrooms places on the Internet where people can post messages and receive instant replies from other people logged onto the site

click through going straight to another web site by clicking on a hyper-link

clipart images (usually line drawings) that can be added to documents

cookies tiny packets of information stored on a customer's computer to provide the business with feedback

customerization   custom design for individual customer's needs

cyber-sitting   when someone buys a domain name with the intention either of preventing someone else from using it or of selling it for a profit

discussion forum   an area on a web site where visitors can post questions or comments and expect replies

dub, dub, dub   the shortened version for the 'www' prefix to web URLs

e-electronic   can be (and often is) used to prefix almost anything: e-commerce, e-business, e-tailing etc.

E2E   electronic market place to electronic market place

e-business   any business transaction carried out electronically

e-commerce   the interrelationship between buyer and seller; commercial interchange

e-enabled   a business's ability to buy and sell or complete other business and commercial transactions through electronic means

EM   Electronic Marketplace   a virtual market place for buying and selling

e-mall   an electronic shop front where you can open a 'stall'

extranet   a private network running over the Internet

e-zines   online magazines

FAQ   Frequently Asked Questions   the section on a web site that attempts to answer customers' queries

firewalls   a barrier between two parts of the web which requires security clearance to pass through and which protects against unauthorized access

flaming   when as many hits as possible are made on a web site in a short space of time in an attempt to crash it

font   the computer term for a typeface; a style of lettering

FTP   File Transfer Protocol   the way to get your site onto its host

GIF   a graphical image format, a way to save a picture or image

hardware and software   both essential to the operation of a computer system; the 'layered model' shows the levels in a system

home page   the first page of your site, an important point which most visitors will come to first

HTML HyperText Mark-up Language, the computer language of web pages

hub the centre to which network devices can be connected

hyper-links 'buttons' that take a user directly to another page

ICANN Internet Corporation for Assigned Names and Numbers

information superhighway the term used to describe the amount of information available on the Internet

Internet the global network of computers which carries out a number of functions including electronic communications, file transfer, and the hosting of the World Wide Web

intranet a set of web pages accessible only from within an organization; often used in education to limit the access of pupils to particular material

ISDN Integrated Services Digital Network; phone line capable of transmitting higher volumes of information than standard phone lines

ISP Internet Service Provider

italic fonts that are rendered so that they slope – *like this*

JPEG one of the most common ways to save an image

LAN Local Area Network

Lotus one of the earlier spreadsheets – still good

m-commerce buying and selling through mobile devices such as mobile phones or PDAs

META tags the key words that help search engines categorize your site and searchers to find it

metasearch engine a search engine that searches other search engines

modem modulator/demodulator; the link between computer and telephone line

MS Excel the spreadsheet that is standard on MS Windows packages

navigating finding your way around a web site

netiquette the accepted rules and conventions when conversing online

newsgroups places on the Internet where people can post information, request information and spark discussions; often these are specific to a particular hobby, interest or group of people and are governed by quite strict rules; some chatrooms and newsgroups are 'moderated' – someone checks the content – but many are not

performance specifications   the key features of a computer

peripherals   'add-ons' that make a system better or more efficient, such as printers and scanners

RAM   Random Access Memory – memory where the computer stores information temporarily; the memory empties when the machine is switched off

router   sends and receives data for your network

search engine   a free service provided on the web through which you can look for sites using key words or phrases

sig. line   your signature or identifier in a newsgroup

SMS   Short Messaging Service, often referred to as text messaging

spreadsheet   will carry out calculations and produce graphs and statistics

thumbnail   a small version of a larger or better defined image

TIFF   Tagged Image File Format – a way of saving an image or picture

URL   Universal Resource Locator; your specific home on the web

VAN   Value Added Network, with higher levels of security provided by an ISP

virtual communities   groups of web users who have joined together to share a common purpose

visibility   the ease with which your web site can be found

WAN   Wide Area Network

web invisibility   the phenomenon of establishing a web site and then not receiving the expected number of visitors

web ring   a series of sites sharing a common product or purpose all joined together by hyper-links

web site   a collection of pages, linked together to form a coherent whole

World Wide Web   a series of interlinked information pages

wysiwyg   what you see is what you get – the software will produce a page as you see it on screen

INDEX